FINANCIAL FREEDOM FORMULA

QUIT YOUR JOB AND BUILD MULTIPLE INCOME STREAMS. ACHIEVE TRUE WEALTH THROUGH PASSIVE INCOME, INVESTING, ETFS, REAL ESTATE, CRYPTO, SIDE HUSTLES, AND ONLINE BUSINESS MODELS

LUCAS STERLING

TOP TIER PRESS

Published under the author brand **Tony Lee**

This edition contains material originally published separately as:

Book One: ***Body Language Decoded*** **© 2025 Top Tier Press**

Book Two: ***How to Analyze People and Spot Lies*** **© 2025 Top Tier Press**

CONTENTS

PART ONE
PASSIVE INCOME MASTERY

PART TWO
INVESTING 101

PART ONE

PASSIVE INCOME MASTERY

DITCH THE 9-TO-5 AND UNLOCK FINANCIAL FREEDOM THROUGH ROYALTIES, STOCKS, CRYPTO, RENTALS, REITS, DROPSHIPPING, YOUTUBE, COURSES, DIGITAL PRODUCTS, AND MORE

INTRODUCTION

What if your bank account quietly grew while you slept, traveled the world, or spent precious moments with loved ones? Imagine waking up to more money than when you went to bed — not because of a promotion or an extra shift, but because you built smart systems that work for you around the clock. For most people, this sounds like a distant dream reserved for lottery winners or tech prodigies. Society has conditioned us to believe that wealth is earned only through relentless effort — sacrificing evenings and weekends in the name of productivity. Yet there's another way — one that doesn't depend on luck, nonstop hustle, or unrealistic promises. This book will show you how passive income can become a practical, achievable path to financial independence.

My name is Lucas Sterling, and I didn't grow up wealthy. My journey began in a small town where my parents worked multiple jobs just to make ends meet. I vividly remember the anxiety that came with every bill and the heavy belief that success was always out of reach. For years, I chased security the traditional way — working harder, taking overtime, and accepting that exhaustion was the price of survival. Then I discovered a simple truth: real freedom isn't earned by adding more hours to your day but by building smart systems that create value long after the work is done. That realization changed everything, and it's the driving force behind this book. The principles and strategies you'll find here aren't abstract theory or empty motivation — they're hard-won lessons from experience, battle-tested models, and practical tools that have helped me and many others build lasting prosperity.

Before we begin this journey, it's crucial to clarify what passive income really means — and to dispel the myths that surround it. Passive income isn't a get-rich-quick scheme or a promise of effortless wealth. The internet is full of scams claiming "overnight success" and easy riches, but let me be clear: that's not what you'll find here. True passive income is built by investing time, resources, or expertise upfront to create assets or systems that require minimal ongoing effort. Think of earning royalties from a book you wrote once or collecting rent from a well-managed property. Compare that to active income, which demands constant labor — salaries, hourly wages, or freelance work that all depend on trading your time for money. Even side hustles, while helpful, often keep your income tied to your hours. Passive income, by contrast, breaks that link. It lets you focus on scaling, automating, and optimizing your revenue streams so you can dedicate your energy to what matters most.

Never before has financial resilience been more essential. Economic instability, global uncertainty, and the rapid rise of automation and artificial intelligence are reshaping the job market at unprecedented speed. Modern work culture has left millions exhausted and disillusioned, shattering the illusion that a single paycheck guarantees stability. As traditional employment grows less secure, building a diversified income portfolio is no longer optional — it's vital. Passive income offers more than financial reward; it provides autonomy over your time, your location, and your choices. It serves as a safety net when markets fluctuate, industries evolve, or life delivers the unexpected. Most importantly, it empowers you to design a future on your own terms — whether that means traveling the world, launching a business, or simply having more time for the people you love.

If you've ever felt trapped in the endless trade of time for money, this book is for you. Maybe you dream of escaping the rigid nine-to-five, exploring new places, or supporting your loved ones without sacrificing your well-being. You may have no experience with investing or entrepreneurship — but if you have ambition and a willingness to learn, you're in the right place. Whether you're an aspiring entrepreneur eager to test ideas, a salaried employee longing for independence, a freelancer seeking stability, a digital nomad craving freedom, or a parent, student, or professional looking for a smarter way forward, you'll find both guidance and encouragement within these pages.

In the chapters ahead, you'll learn to identify and create passive income streams that match your skills, interests, and resources. We'll explore how to earn royalties from writing, music, and digital content; invest wisely in stocks, cryptocurrencies, and real estate investment trusts (REITs); generate stable rental income through strategic property management; build dropshipping and e-commerce ventures; automate YouTube channels for steady ad revenue; and develop online courses and digital products that continue to pay long after they're made. You'll also learn how to stack, scale, and diversify these income streams into a resilient portfolio — one that stands strong through economic shifts and market cycles.

This book is designed to be as practical as possible. Perfection isn't required. You don't need to master every method or pursue them all at once. Instead, choose one income stream that aligns with your strengths and situation, and take the first concrete step. If you have a specific goal, skip ahead to the chapter that resonates with you. Each section includes actionable summaries, simple checklists, and curated tools to accelerate your progress and eliminate guesswork. Every chapter ends with clear steps you can apply right away, so you're never left wondering what to do next.

Financial freedom doesn't depend on luck, privilege, or advanced technical skills. Anyone, regardless of background or education, can learn to build sustainable, diversified income streams. It simply requires structure, patience, and the courage to take action. begin. My goal is to give you the knowledge, frameworks, and confidence to design your own path, one that leads not only to wealth but also to genuine freedom and fulfillment.

Now is the time to reclaim control of your financial life. Let's build your independence, one income stream at a time.

UNLOCK YOUR FINANCIAL FREEDOM BLUEPRINT

Ready to turn your financial goals into real, actionable progress?

As a thank-you for reading this book, I've created a powerful companion resource: **The Financial Freedom Blueprint**. This exclusive, step-by-step guide helps you identify your ideal money path, plug income leaks, and make smart, aligned decisions fast. It's designed to take you from financial confusion to confidence in just a few focused steps.

What's included in this resource:

- Clarify your goals
- Streamline your expenses
- Align your spending with your values
- Start building real wealth now!

👉 **Access Your Financial Blueprint Today**

Visit: **https://content.toptierpress.com/unlock-financial-freedom**

Or scan the QR code below to get instant access!

ONE
THE FOUNDATIONS OF PASSIVE INCOME

Many people dream of earning money while they sleep, picturing a life free from the daily grind of a traditional job. The idea of passive income, money that flows in with little ongoing effort, has captured the imagination of aspiring entrepreneurs and professionals alike. Nevertheless, for many, this vision remains elusive. Despite sincere intentions and hard work, countless individuals struggle to build income streams that truly operate without constant attention. They discover themselves caught between misconceptions and reality, unsure why their efforts don't translate into lasting financial freedom.

The challenge lies not only in understanding what passive income really means but also in recognizing how it differs from the active work most are familiar with. Many attempt quick fixes or chase "easy" opportunities, only to encounter setbacks, confusion, or burnout. Success requires more than just starting; it demands patience, strategy, and a mindset shift toward long-term thinking.

This chapter explores the foundations of passive income by defining its true nature, contrasting it with active income, and revealing common pitfalls that cause many to fail. It then guides readers toward adopting the mindset needed to navigate their passive income journey effectively. By developing realistic expectations and embracing a builder's mindset, anyone can begin to lay the groundwork for sustainable, scalable income streams that contribute to genuine financial independence.

UNDERSTANDING PASSIVE INCOME: DEFINITIONS, CHARACTERISTICS, AND KEY DIFFERENCES

Passive income is the money you earn with little or no daily effort to maintain or grow it after the initial setup. Its core features include recurring revenue, minimal maintenance requirements, and the potential for scalability. Understanding these aspects is the first step to seeing why passive income attracts so much attention and why it's often misunderstood.

Recurring revenue is the backbone of genuine passive income. Instead of one-off payments, this income flows into your account repeatedly, whether you're working currently or not. For example, an author receives book royalties every time a copy sells, even years after writing it. Investors collect dividends from stocks regularly, and landlords earn rental income from tenants month after month. These streams share the common trait of persistence, once established, money keeps coming without needing to restart the process.

The minimal maintenance required is what sets passive income apart from most side hustles or jobs. You might spend time upfront creating a digital product such as an ebook or a set of templates. Once launched online, sales, delivery, and customer service can run automatically through e-commerce systems or third-party marketplaces. This frees you from daily management and repetitive tasks, allowing you to focus on new projects or simply enjoy the results.

Scalability is the key that unlocks greater financial independence through passive income. Unlike traditional work, where earnings are tied to hours worked, scalable passive income allows one piece of effort to generate returns again and again, no matter how many people purchase it. Imagine designing an online course. The upfront work is significant — writing lessons, editing videos, and building a sales page

— but once complete, it can educate dozens or even thousands of students, earning income from each one without additional labor.

Many people encounter myths about passive income that distort their expectations. Some believe it's instant and effortless — that you can set up something today and start earning tomorrow. The truth is different. All genuine passive income sources require effort, skill, or capital at the beginning. An author spends months writing a book before receiving royalties. A landlord invests time and money securing property before collecting rent.

Another common myth is that passive income is risk-free. In reality, every passive income source carries some level of risk. Book sales can fizzle out, rental properties may sit vacant or need repairs, and even dividend-paying stocks can lose value or be affected by market swings. Each opportunity demands thoughtful research, ongoing monitoring, and a willingness to adapt.

There's also confusion about what activities count as passive income. Let's clarify the differences:

Income Type	Maintenance Level	Example
True Passive	Very Low	Rental property managed by a company
Semi-Passive	Low to Moderate	Blog needing periodic content updates
Active Marketed as Passive	High	Day trading or gig work with inconsistent results

True passive income, like a rental property managed by professionals, lets your investment work with minimal input. In contrast, a blog that brings ad revenue can seem passive, but needs fresh content, updates, and marketing. Day trading, sometimes promoted as the ultimate freedom-generating strategy, is in fact highly time-consuming. It requires near-constant attention and exposes you to significant risk, making it active work rather than genuine passive income.

To grasp the distinction further, consider the time-for-money relationship:

- With active income (like freelancing), every dollar earned reflects time spent working. Miss a day, lose a day's pay.
- With passive income, your effort is concentrated at the beginning. Write a book or build a course today, and you might reap earnings automatically for years to come. An initial push combined with patience brings ongoing rewards.

For aspiring entrepreneurs and professionals, this shift means thinking in longer timelines. It can take months or even a few years before passive income streams reliably grow and start covering living expenses. Building true passive income requires dedication to creating value upfront, a willingness to learn from challenges, and the patience to see your investments pay off over time.

The journey to passive income isn't always easy, and it's not void of effort at any stage. But the advantage is clear: instead of exchanging hours for dollars indefinitely, you're building assets that can grant you greater freedom and security. Success in passive income comes down to adopting a strategic mindset, focusing on sustainable growth, and seeking opportunities that match your skills and resources. Letting go of "quick win" fantasies and embracing realistic expectations sets the foundation for genuine financial independence and a more flexible future.

THE PSYCHOLOGY OF SUCCESS: OVERCOMING PITFALLS AND SHIFTING TO A BUILDER'S MINDSET

The dream of passive income often falters at the starting line, not because earning money outside of a traditional job is impossible, but because of how people approach the journey. At the heart of most failures is impatience. Many enter the world of passive income expecting results in weeks or months, influenced by loud promises of "overnight success" from social media or online ads. When the early effort produces little or nothing, discouragement takes over. Imagine someone who launches an affiliate website, checks their earnings after only a month, and, seeing a balance of $5, decides it's not worth the hassle. This impatience leads them to abandon what could have become a steady, profitable stream.

Unrealistic expectations often feed this impatience. The idea that passive income means "no work" is widespread but dangerously misleading. Building a successful YouTube channel, for example, requires months, often years, of creating, refining, learning from feedback, and persisting through low view counts. The allure of skipping this grind is strong; so many people flit from one "hot" opportunity to another, never staying the course long enough to see real growth.

This lack of focus is another major downfall. It's easy, in today's world, to jump from dropshipping to real estate wholesaling to digital courses and back again. With every switch, valuable time and attention get diverted; instead of mastering the details of one business, people become dabblers. Resources are spread thin; you cannot properly analyze a rental property, edit a video series, and manage a Shopify store all at once. Real growth happens through deep work, not shallow dabbling.

Another stumbling block comes from within: overthinking and fear of making mistakes. Many would-be creators get stuck "perfecting" their product forever. Consider Priya, an instructional designer who spends six months refining her online course, tirelessly editing and re-recording. She reads forums, tweaks video quality, polishes slides, and second-guesses pricing but never launches. She ends up with a polished course no one ever sees. Similarly, there's David, who has studied rental property investing for years, analyzing hundreds of listings but never making an offer. Both are trapped by analysis paralysis, never turning learning into action.

Each of these barriers is surmountable. First, changing expectations is crucial. Sustainable passive income almost always begins with small steps, not grand gestures. "Small" can mean launching a minimum viable product, a seven-page ebook instead of a full masterclass, or renting out one spare room instead of buying an entire apartment complex. Small projects are less risky, easier to manage, and faster to deliver. Early wins build confidence and provide data for improvement.

Focusing on one stream at a time brings significant benefits. Concentrating on a single project makes it far easier to learn fast, iterate, and develop expertise. For instance, Mia decides to start with print-on-demand T-shirts. She creates ten basic designs, sets a goal to make her first sale within 30 days, and tracks daily traffic to her online store. Once sales become steady, she considers branching out. This sharp focus accelerates learning, keeps tasks manageable, and leads to more meaningful results.

Consistency is essential, but it needs to be defined by practical, measurable actions. Instead of vague commitments, successful builders set clear milestones: uploading one new YouTube video per week, running five product ads daily, or submitting three new real estate offers per month. These micro-goals pile up over time. Luca, who saw no rental income for his first six months, remained committed to analyzing five properties a week and submitting two offers each month. It took nine months to close his first deal, but by then, his habits and skills were solidified.

Success in passive income also comes from thinking like a builder or owner, not just a consumer. The consumer mentality seeks entertainment, easy answers, and quick rewards. Builders investigate how to solve problems and create value, even when the initial payoff is invisible. This shift can be practiced by making tiny decisions: writing instead of scrolling social media, following up with leads instead of waiting for them, or choosing to learn a new skill with direct application. Over time, this mindset becomes second nature.

Linking passive income goals to personal values keeps motivation strong through setbacks. Melissa, a busy parent, connects her pursuit of rental income to her desire for flexible family time. When obstacles arise, she remembers her deeper purpose, which fuels her discipline to keep going when progress feels slow. Powerful passive income efforts are always grounded in clear, personal reasons that outlast temporary frustrations.

Success is not about perfect timing or flawless execution but about starting small, staying focused, acting consistently, and building with intention.

Now that we have clarified what passive income truly entails, how it differs from active income, and the common obstacles that hinder success, readers will be equipped to approach this journey with a realistic and patient mindset. Building sustainable passive income requires focused effort, consistent action, and a willingness to learn and adapt over time. By setting clear goals, concentrating on one opportunity at a time, and aligning efforts with personal values, aspiring entrepreneurs can overcome challenges and gradually create reliable income streams that provide greater financial freedom. Embracing this builder's mindset positions you not just to earn money passively but to build lasting assets that support long-term independence and flexibility beyond the traditional work model.

TWO
SETTING YOUR FINANCIAL FREEDOM GOAL

Imagine waking each day without the pressure of a rigid schedule or without financial stress dictating your choices. For some, this freedom means pursuing passions long set aside; for others, it represents security and flexibility to spend time with family or explore new ventures. Yet despite these varied visions, many aspiring entrepreneurs and professionals struggle to define what true financial independence looks like for themselves. Without a clear target, the path to sustained income beyond the traditional job can feel uncertain and overwhelming.

This chapter guides you in discovering your unique vision of financial freedom by reflecting on what matters most in your life. It will help you calculate a personalized "freedom number", the monthly amount needed to support your ideal lifestyle and develop practical methods to track your progress. By connecting your mindset with measurable financial goals, you create a foundation that supports consistent growth in multiple income streams. Through building effective budgeting habits and sustaining motivation, you prepare yourself not just to dream about financial independence but to take deliberate, focused steps toward achieving it.

CLARIFYING YOUR PERSONAL FINANCIAL FREEDOM AND CALCULATING YOUR FREEDOM NUMBER

Imagine one person's financial freedom means stepping away from boardrooms to start a rescue center for stray animals. For someone else, it might mean never feeling rushed in the morning, sipping homemade coffee on their balcony with loved ones nearby. Each person's blueprint feels different, because freedom doesn't have a single form. Consider Maria, who led major corporate teams for years but felt her real purpose was launching a nonprofit focused on literacy. Her freedom looks like early meetings with passionate volunteers and afternoons organizing book drives, with more time for her teenage children at home. In another scenario, Sam teaches high school science but dreams of running an online tutoring business from anywhere in the world. He pictures exploring new countries every few months, his laptop his only office. Then there's Jasmine and David, raising two kids in a lively suburb; they see financial independence as stress-free college funds, family trips to national parks, and enough flexibility for David to transition from a demanding tech job into freelance consulting.

These stories show that financial independence isn't a fixed destination; it's about creating a life shaped by your values, preferences, and dreams. Instead of keeping up with external expectations, you define what truly matters.

A powerful way to discover your personal vision is through a guided visualization exercise. Choose a quiet spot. Sit, close your eyes, and breathe deeply. Imagine your best day after you've achieved financial freedom. What time do you wake up? Who are you with? Where do you live? How do you spend your time throughout the day, from your morning coffee to your evening relaxation? Do you work on creative projects, travel, or focus on relationships? Notice the sounds, textures, colors, and the overall mood of your ideal day. Ask yourself: What activities fill you with purpose? Which moments bring you peace or excitement? What do you never want to go back to? Next, reflect on the feelings this ideal day evokes. Write down words that describe your mood: calm, joyful, energized, relieved. Then consider what these insights suggest about your real priorities. List three or four realizations or unexpected desires that stand out. Finally, review your notes and record the key details in a notebook or digital document. They're your personal North Star for shaping your freedom plan.

Turning vision into tangible action starts with knowing exactly what you need each month to make it real: a concrete "freedom number." Here's how to pinpoint yours, step by step.

1. Make a table of all your fixed monthly expenses. These might include rent or mortgage, utilities, insurance, car payments, cell phone bills, and healthcare premiums.
2. List variable costs — groceries, transportation, dining out, entertainment, hobbies, clothing, and personal care.
3. Add line items for the upgrades you'd love — occasional weekend trips, new tech gear, fitness classes, more shows or concerts, or that upgraded streaming bundle.
4. Consider contributions to savings, retirement, or investment accounts for long-term security.
5. Finally, add a 20% buffer to protect your lifestyle if emergencies or one-off expenses pop up.

Example Table: Freedom Number Calculation

Category	Minimalist Nomad	Suburban Family	Urban Professional
Housing/utilities	$1,400	$2,800	$3,500
Food	$400	$1,200	$1,100
Transportation	$200	$800	$500
Insurance/healthcare	$250	$750	$600
Lifestyle/upgrades	$400	$1,000	$2,200
Savings/investing	$200	$750	$1,000
Entertainment	$150	$400	$850
Education/other	•	$550	$550
20% Security buffer	$600	$1,300	$2,000
Total/Month	**$3,000**	**$8,000**	**$12,000**

For Jamie, the minimalist nomad, home is a series of short-term rentals across Southeast Asia. Fixed costs include $900 for accommodation, $500 for food, and modest insurance premiums. Jamie values flexibility and adventure over luxury. Savings and upgrade buckets allow for monthly treks and online learning. Their freedom number, including the buffer, totals $3,000.

The Carters, living in a suburban neighborhood, need consistency for their kids' schooling and activities. Their $2,500 mortgage supports a comfortable home base. Utilities and groceries run higher, plus sports and music for the children. They want vacations and bigger family outings. Aiming for $8,000 monthly gives them confidence to invest in their future.

Priya, the urban professional, lives in a downtown condo, walking to a favorite bistro on weekends. She enjoys theater, fitness studios, and robust savings for early retirement. High housing costs, elevated utility bills, health and wellness extras, and creative pursuits make her monthly freedom number $12,000 — with a comfortable buffer for surprises.

Your freedom number comes from these choices — what you value, where you thrive, and how you wish to grow. It isn't just covering needs; it should leave space for security, upgrades, and future plans. Remember, passive income from investments or ventures will help reach this target, but for now, focus on defining what that target is. There are no wrong answers — only the answer that lines up with your vision.

BUILDING TRACKING HABITS, BUDGETING EFFECTIVELY, AND SUSTAINING MOTIVATION

Creating a system for tracking your finances builds a solid structure for reaching your passive income goals. By maintaining clear records, you gain financial clarity that leads to better decisions — the kind that help you spot opportunities and avoid costly mistakes. When your ultimate goal is your freedom number, each tracked dollar works as a stepping stone toward that exact target.

Manual spreadsheet tracking offers a simple, accessible method to take control of your finances. This approach uses a basic spreadsheet to log every income source and expense. Most people begin by listing all inflows and outflows on a weekly or monthly basis. To implement this, set up columns for date, category, amount, and notes. Each time you spend or earn, record the transaction right away. For a side hustler, this could mean entering every purchase tied to startup supplies, while a professional might note dividend payments or stock sales. An entrepreneur juggling multiple projects can create a tab for each income stream to isolate trends. The main pitfalls with spreadsheets involve missing small purchases, getting behind on updates, or neglecting to categorize entries accurately. If you find yourself making decisions with up-to-date information, detecting overspending early, and feeling confident about your trajectory, your manual tracking is working.

Basic budgeting apps offer an intermediate level of systemization. These programs automate much of the data entry by syncing with your bank accounts and credit cards. After setup, you allocate transactions into categories and assess spending against custom budgets. Side hustlers benefit from separating business and personal flows in the app for tax preparation. Professionals tracking investment returns can set notifications for incoming dividends or changes in portfolio value. Entrepreneurs see cash flow for several ventures in one dashboard. Implementation involves downloading an app, securely connecting accounts, and categorizing at least weekly to avoid errors. Some users fall into the trap of ignoring app notifications, leading to blind spots, or relying too much on automatic categorization, which can mislabel purchases. When your app shows accurate balances, categorization matches your goals, and your freedom number's gap narrows month-to-month, your tracking is on target.

Comprehensive financial platforms represent the advanced method. These solutions integrate banking, investments, budgeting, and even tax planning in one interface. After you onboard all accounts — checking, savings, brokerage, and any business holdings — the software generates detailed reports and forecasts. A side hustler uses platform analytics to track profitability, factoring in both expenses and varied income streams. A professional monitors shifting asset allocations, dividend yield, and tax-loss harvesting. The multi-venture entrepreneur benefits from consolidated reporting on personal, business, and passive income streams. Implementing these tools involves regular review sessions, setting up custom reports, and using alerts for key events, such as dips below your target investment rate. The biggest mistakes with platforms include setup overload, ignoring data analysis, or failing to act on insights. If you consistently receive actionable recommendations, see progress toward your freedom number in your dashboards, and notice fewer surprises in your finances, your system is paying off.

Use the 70/20/10 budgeting framework to build a realistic and robust financial foundation. Assign 70% of your monthly after-tax income to living expenses, 20% to investments, and 10% to savings. This arrangement ensures living costs remain sustainable while you reserve a full fifth of your income for building passive assets. Saving 10% creates a buffer against emergencies or missed income. For example, if your current expense tracking shows $3,000 per month, the framework suggests no more than $2,100 for living costs, $600 for investments, and $300 directed strictly to savings. By sticking to this breakdown, you architect your finances specifically for long-term freedom.

For a practical step, dedicate a week to logging every expense. Review receipts and bank statements to classify spending as needs or wants, such as housing and groceries versus streaming subscriptions and takeout. Calculate your current percentage of income going to investments. Compare your habits to the 70/20/10 framework by constructing a simple table:

Category	Current Allocation	Framework Target	Difference
Living Expenses	$2,500 (83%)	$2,100 (70%)	+$400
Investments	$350 (12%)	$600 (20%)	-$250
Savings	$150 (5%)	$300 (10%)	-$150

Identify excesses in living costs or areas where investment contributions fall short. Reallocate funds accordingly to optimize progress.

Motivation grows when you connect everyday habits to visible progress. Develop a simple monitoring system where you track milestones like meeting your monthly passive income goal, hitting a new investment diversification benchmark, reducing monthly discretionary expenses, and increasing your freedom number buffer. Healthy progress might look like achieving a $100 increase in monthly passive income or lowering grocery bills by $50 through meal planning. Avoid demotivating comparisons such as measuring your pace against online personalities.

Anchor your system with habits that make tracking sustainable: schedule a weekly review of accounts, adapt goals during a monthly check-in, celebrate quarterly achievements such as your first $1,000 in passive income, and revisit your overall strategy each year. This structure keeps your financial foundation strong and your eyes focused on the next stage — putting your tracking to work in building real, recurring passive income.

Having now defined your unique vision of financial freedom, calculated your personalized freedom number, and established a practical framework for tracking and budgeting, you are equipped to take intentional steps toward your goals. With clarity on what matters most to you and a realistic action plan rooted in disciplined habits, you can confidently build and grow multiple streams of passive income. Embracing this tailored approach empowers you to move beyond uncertainty, steadily closing the gap between your current reality and the life you envision. As you implement these strategies, your focus will sharpen, motivation will strengthen, and each small milestone will bring you closer to lasting financial independence and the freedom to live on your own terms.

THREE
EARNING FROM ROYALTIES AND INTELLECTUAL PROPERTY

Have you ever wondered how some creators manage to earn money long after their work is finished? Imagine writing a book, composing music, or creating art once and then receiving payments on that effort for months or even years without additional active work. This idea of generating income from intellectual property — spreading your creative output across different formats and platforms — is something many aspire to but few fully understand.

Turning creativity, knowledge, or expertise into a steady stream of royalties offers a way to build financial independence beyond the usual paycheck-to-paycheck cycle. It requires not only producing quality content but also knowing how to leverage publishing tools, distribution channels, and legal protections. The potential lies in creating assets that continue to earn through multiple formats like ebooks, audiobooks, translations, and prints, which can expand reach and diversify earnings over time. In this chapter, we will examine the foundations of royalty income and intellectual property, exploring how to transform your work into scalable, recurring revenue sources while safeguarding your rights.

MONETIZING BOOKS, MUSIC, PHOTOGRAPHY, AND ART

Aspiring authors and creators leverage royalty-based income streams by publishing digital books, print-on-demand paperbacks, and audiobooks on major platforms. Amazon Kindle Direct Publishing (KDP) leads the self-publishing landscape for ebooks and paperbacks, providing broad market access and transparent royalty models. KDP allows authors to upload manuscripts in formats like DOCX or PDF through a clear, step-by-step dashboard. The interface displays fields for book title, author name, description, categories, and keywords. When uploading a manuscript, KDP's preview tool reveals how the finished ebook or paperback will appear on Kindle devices and in print. The royalty structure for ebooks is straightforward: authors set list prices between $2.99 and $9.99 to access a 70% royalty rate (minus a small delivery fee) in eligible regions. For paperbacks, royalties are set at 60% of the list price minus printing costs, typically around $2.15 for a standard black-and-white US print.

In contrast, audiobooks are distributed via Audible ACX and Findaway Voices. Audiobook production can require more upfront investment but offers unique income channels. ACX, Audible's own platform, enables authors to recruit narrators, pay per finished hour, or split royalties. ACX pays 40% royalties for exclusive distribution to Audible, Amazon, and iTunes, or 25% for non-exclusive distribution. Findaway Voices provides access to more retailers but offers a flat 45% royalty from sales, with broader reach. Both platforms require completed audio files, standardized opening/closing credits, a retail sample, and adherence to quality requirements such as specific bit rates and RMS levels.

Successful authors who publish across these formats illustrate the potential of self-publishing. For example, Mark Dawson, a thriller novelist, consistently reports six-figure annual royalties from his KDP titles, amplified by effective email marketing and advertising. Rachel Morgan, a young adult author, gained traction with a focused fantasy niche, reporting royalties of $7,000–$10,000 per month from combined ebook, paperback, and audiobook sales. Earnings vary; a single well-performing ebook series can generate $20,000–$100,000 per year, while a top-selling audiobook can add another $5,000–$50,000, provided that content reaches a sizable audience and maintains high review scores.

Choosing content with long-term earning potential starts with researching evergreen topics and niche opportunities. Use Amazon's bestseller charts, keyword research tools like Publisher Rocket, and competitor analysis to identify categories with steady demand and low-to-moderate competition. Search for topics with consistent ranks in the Kindle Store's top 1,000 or those with thousands of existing reviews but little recent release activity. To validate a topic, estimate monthly sales using the Amazon Best Sellers Rank (BSR) to earnings calculators; for example, a title ranked #5,000 in Kindle may sell 200–300 copies per month.

Efficient content creation combines structured writing, high editing standards, and production support. Many successful authors outsource parts of the process. Ghostwriters charge $0.03–$0.15 per word based on experience and genre, while editors cost $300–$1,200 per manuscript depending on length and depth of service (developmental vs. copy editing). Professional cover designers range from $50 to $300, and AI-assisted tools like Grammarly, ProWritingAid, and Sudowrite streamline grammar, tone, and style checks. Budgeting $1,000–$2,500 for full production and marketing is typical for first-time publishers seeking strong results.

Quality control is essential. KDP and ACX provide precise formatting requirements: EPUB for ebooks, print-ready PDFs for paperbacks, and structured WAV or MP3 files for audiobooks. All platforms demand clearly defined metadata — titles, subtitles, categories, keywords — that maximize discoverability. Metadata optimization includes focusing on genre keywords, search intent, and accurate category selection. Writing compelling and concise book descriptions directly shapes conversion rates.

Pricing strategies combine competitive list pricing, limited-time promotions, and strategic series bundling. Many authors experiment with Amazon's Kindle Countdown Deals or free promotions to gather early reviews and boost initial visibility. Audiobooks, with price points ranging from $9.99 to $29.99, include options like Audible's credit and subscription systems, which can affect payout consistency.

Marketing fundamentals revolve around building email lists, reader engagement, and leveraging Amazon Ads or BookBub campaigns to drive traffic. Tracking sales, download data, and royalty statements in real-time dashboards provides immediate insights for adjusting strategies. Comparing options, KDP offers higher ebook royalties and visibility, while ACX/Findaway capture audio listeners seeking premium content.

Initial publishing might take 1–3 months, depending on content complexity and service availability. Upfront costs represent a risk, but careful niche selection, consistent quality, and attentive marketing lower the chance of unprofitability. Once content is launched, royalties provide truly passive income. Content translated into new languages and repurposed across ebook, print, and audio formats amplifies reach and diversifies revenue even further.

EXPANDING REVENUE STREAMS AND PROTECTING YOUR WORK

When a creator understands the power of format multiplication, a single content asset can produce steady, diversified revenue streams. For example, consider a self-published entrepreneur who launched a practical business guide. Initial earnings came from ebook and paperback sales via Amazon KDP and IngramSpark, generating $450 monthly — 70% from ebook, 30% paperback. In the second month, they produced an audiobook using ACX, investing $300 in narration, and released across Audible, Apple Books, and Google Play. Audiobook sales contributed an additional $320 monthly, with Audible representing 80% of those royalties. By month four, the book was translated into Spanish and German (each translation averaging $700 and three weeks to complete), distributed via Draft2Digital and Kobo Writing Life, and promoted through region-specific Amazon ads and Spanish-language podcast sponsorships. These editions averaged $180 monthly per translated market, bringing total monthly income above $1,000 and consistently growing.

Creators follow a process built on strategic planning and platform knowledge. After establishing the original format, expand reach by offering audiobook versions — either by narrating personally or through professional talent. Major platforms, such as ACX, offer 40% royalty for exclusive distribution and 25% for non-exclusive. Extend further with translations using reputable freelancers via Reedsy or Babelcube. Royalties on Babelcube, for instance, begin at 30%, rising to 85% after $2,000 in sales. Market these adaptations through targeted ads, coordinated launch campaigns, and territory-focused partnerships. This multi-format approach not only multiplies income but also strengthens brand presence across diverse segments.

Format Multiplication Planning

Take these direct steps:

- Write your primary content asset (e.g., an English-language small business starter guide)
- Identify three format transformations:
  a. Audiobook version ($300 narration cost, projected monthly sales: $250)
  b. The Spanish ebook and print-on-demand (POD) release will incur a translation cost of $700, with projected monthly sales estimated at $120.
  c. The German audiobook has a translation and narration cost of $900, with projected monthly sales of $130.

- Calculate potential revenue: (Ebook $400) + (Audiobook $250) + (Spanish $120) + (German $130) = $900/mo
- Create a 6-month timeline:
  - Month 1: Ebook/Paperback launch
  - Month 2: Audiobook production and release
  - Month 3–4: Spanish translation and publication
  - Month 5: Spanish audiobook or next language expansion
  - Month 6: German publication and marketing

This plan transforms a single content asset into a multi-stream earning engine within 180 days.

Legal Protections in Format Expansion

Every format multiplied must be protected by clear, proactive legal actions. Copyright registration in your primary jurisdiction provides legal proof and damages eligibility in infringement claims. In the US, you can register a single work within 90 days of its publication on copyright.gov for $65 through electronic filing. Internationally, rely on the Berne Convention's automatic protection, but always verify local requirements in new markets.

Clear contracts are essential when commissioning translations, audiobook productions, or designer collaborations. A strong contract details work-for-hire status (if applicable), payment, delivery deadlines, rights assignment, and territory coverage. Determine usage rights at the start — do you want exclusive or non-exclusive rights? Platforms such as ACX require contractual confirmation of distribution rights and territory specifics. When expanding into print, assign your ISBN through Bowker ($125 for a block of 10 ISBNs in the US), and file for copyright registration.

Legal Protection Framework

Apply these direct steps:

- File copyright registration at copyright.gov within 90 days; retain the completion certificate.
- Draw up contracts listing rights, deliverables, scope, and payment; review for completeness.
- Decide on licensing and usage rights per format: assign exclusive rights for audiobooks or translations if higher royalties are offered.
- Check each platform's legal requirements; on Spotify or Apple Music, music requires mechanical and performance rights clearance (managed via Harry Fox Agency or BMI, $75 setup and variable royalty rates). For art, clarify licensing terms —

e.g., one-time fee vs. royalty percentage, duration, and territories.

- For books: obtain ISBN, file copyright, attach clear contracts with collaborators.
- For music: register with PRO (ASCAP, BMI), obtain mechanical licenses, maintain explicit distributor contracts.
- For visual art: draft licensing agreements, state usage restrictions, document any exclusive rights granted.

IP Protection Audit

Follow this practical implementation:

- List all current IP assets and their legal registration status.
- Spot any assets without copyright registration, lack of contracts, or unclear ownership.
- Take action: register copyrights online today, draft missing contracts, and renegotiate any ambiguous terms.
- Organize documentation: certificates, executed contracts, platform receipts, and email confirmations in digital files.

One entrepreneur, starting with a single small business guide, earned $450/mo from sales. Format expansion (audiobook, Spanish/German editions) doubled monthly revenue in six months. Copyright filing within three weeks of launch deterred pirated online editions. Each contract for translation assigned exclusive language rights, with automated royalty splits managed via Babelcube and ACX. ISBN assignment for every print edition ensured global tracking and retail eligibility.

This section empowers creators to multiply their intellectual property's income while securing their future earnings. The upcoming downloadable "IP Income Starter Kit" checklist gives you every tool to put these strategies into action.

Now that you understand how to harness the power of royalty-based income and intellectual property, you can begin transforming your knowledge, creativity, or expertise into scalable and recurring revenue streams. By strategically creating content across multiple formats; e-books, audiobooks, translations, and print editions, and securing your rights through proper legal protections, you set the foundation for sustainable passive income that grows over time. With careful planning, quality production, and targeted marketing, you can multiply your earnings, expand your reach globally, and build a diversified portfolio that moves you closer to financial independence. Embracing these methods empowers you to break free from traditional income limitations and confidently shape a future defined by ongoing, automated returns on your intellectual investments.

FOUR
BUILDING WEALTH THROUGH STOCKS AND DIVIDENDS

Have you ever wondered how some people manage to create a steady flow of income without having to clock in every day? Many dream of building financial security that works quietly in the background, supporting their goals without constant effort or expertise. Yet for those unfamiliar with investing, especially the complexities of the stock market, this idea can feel overwhelming or out of reach.

The world of stocks often seems exclusive to experts or wealthy individuals, and the idea of earning money just by owning shares seems unreal. Questions arise: How do dividends actually work? Can someone without a finance background really build wealth through stocks? And what steps can turn this passive income into a reliable source over time? This chapter will guide you through understanding dividend investing and how it can serve as a cornerstone in creating a sustainable income portfolio. With clear explanations and practical insights, it aims to empower you to navigate the stock market confidently and develop a long-term strategy for growing your wealth steadily and securely.

FOUNDATIONS OF DIVIDEND INVESTING AND BUILDING A MONTHLY INCOME PORTFOLIO

Dividend investing offers a way for individuals to build wealth by receiving a share of company profits as cash payments. These payments, known as dividends, are typically paid quarterly, but some companies may distribute them monthly or annually. When you own stock in a company that pays dividends, you receive regular deposits of money, usually credited directly to your brokerage account. Companies known for steady dividends include giants like Coca-Cola, Johnson & Johnson, and Procter & Gamble. By sharing excess profits with shareholders, these businesses signal financial health and a long-term commitment to returning value.

Dividends are not guaranteed, but many established companies aim to maintain or raise their payouts year after year. For example, if you own 100 shares of a company that pays $0.50 per share each quarter, you receive $50 every three months simply for holding your shares. This predictable income stream is attractive to investors seeking stability, such as retirees or those planning for long-term goals. A company's dividend yield, expressed as a percentage, tells you how much annual income you can expect in relation to the stock's current price. For instance, if a stock trades at $50 and pays a $2 annual dividend, its yield is 4%.

An effective way to maximize the power of dividends is through DRIPs, or Dividend Reinvestment Plans. A DRIP automatically uses the cash dividends you receive to purchase more shares of the company instead of depositing the payment in your account. This reinvestment takes place every dividend cycle, harnessing the benefit of compound growth. Compounding means you earn dividends on your original investment as well as previous dividends that have been reinvested, creating a snowball effect over time.

Consider a straightforward example. Imagine investing $1,000 in a company with a 4% annual dividend yield. Without a DRIP, you would receive $40 per year in cash. By enrolling in a DRIP, those $40 buy more shares, which in turn generate further dividends. If the stock price and dividend yield remain constant, the following year you would own $1,040 worth of stock, and your dividend would rise to $41.60. Over multiple years, this compounding accelerates growth — after 10 years, your original $1,000 could grow to approximately $1,480, excluding stock price changes. If the company increases its dividend or the stock appreciates, growth is even more significant.

Dividend investing provides three key advantages. First, it delivers predictable income. Most companies pay on set schedules — quarterly payments are common, meaning you receive income every three months. Some real estate investment trusts (REITs) and special funds may pay monthly. Second, there's long-term growth potential. Many renowned companies, known as "dividend aristocrats," have raised dividends every year for decades. For example, Johnson & Johnson and Coca-Cola have increased dividends annually for over 50 years, rewarding long-term shareholders with rising payouts even during market downturns. Third, dividend investing is appealing for its low-maintenance nature. Once you select reliable dividend payers and enroll in a DRIP, your investment grows automatically with very little ongoing management. You do not need to monitor prices or trade frequently.

Getting started with dividend investing does not require large sums of money. Many brokerage platforms now allow you to buy partial shares with as little as $1. Several offer commission-free trading, making it easy for beginners to start small and grow over time. Here is a comparison of three popular platforms:

Platform	Minimum Investment	Dividends Auto-Reinvestment	User Experience	Unique Feature
Robinhood	$1	Yes (automated)	Simple, fast signup	User-friendly mobile interface
M1 Finance	$10	Yes (customizable pies)	Streamlined, goal-based	Automated portfolio rebalancing
eToro	$10	Yes (with fractional shares)	Social investing tools	CopyTrader (mimic top investors)

Through these platforms, you can research dividend-paying stocks, open a brokerage account, and activate DRIP or reinvestment features on your dashboard. To calculate potential returns, multiply the number of shares owned by the dividend per share for total annual income, or use the dividend yield to estimate returns on your investment. For instance, owning 50 shares of a company that pays $1 per share yearly brings $50 in annual dividends. To estimate compounded growth with DRIP, online calculators can help you factor in reinvested earnings and potential dividend increases.

Dividend investors have the flexibility to choose between individual stocks, such as blue-chip companies, and index funds or ETFs that bundle many dividend-paying stocks together. Index funds, especially those focused on dividends, offer built-in diversification, ease of management, and smoother performance. Individual stocks, on the other hand, allow targeted exposure but require more research and monitoring.

Whether you prefer a set-and-forget approach or want to handpick stocks, you can start building income-generating portfolios with confidence and clarity by understanding these basics and using beginner-friendly tools.

OPTIMIZING TAXES, REINVESTMENT STRATEGIES, AND PRACTICAL TOOLS FOR DIVIDEND INVESTORS

Qualified dividends usually come from shares of large, established companies such as Microsoft (MSFT) or Johnson & Johnson (JNJ). These dividends meet IRS criteria and are taxed at the lower long-term capital gains rates — 0%, 15%, or 20% depending on your income. By contrast, ordinary dividends may arise from real estate investment trusts (REITs), like Realty Income (O), or master limited partnerships (MLPs). These are taxed as regular income, potentially up to 37%. For instance, if you earn $1,000 in qualified dividends from Coca-Cola (KO) and fall into the 15% capital gains bracket, you owe $150 in taxes. An equal $1,000 from a REIT, taxed at your 24% income rate, results in a $240 tax bill. The distinction can significantly affect your after-tax returns.

Dividend Source	Tax Category	Example Stock	Tax Rate (Mid Bracket)	Tax Owed ($1,000)
MSFT, KO	Qualified Dividend	MSFT, KO	15%	$150
Realty Income (O)	Ordinary Dividend	REIT	24%	$240

Common pitfalls involve overloading a taxable brokerage account with high-yielding ordinary dividend stocks, leading to tax bills that erode real returns. Investors often don't consider the asset type's tax impact — holding REITs in a taxable account, for example, rather than inside a tax-sheltered IRA.

To implement an efficient structure:

- First, review each holding's dividend qualities.
- Place qualified dividend stocks in taxable accounts, but prioritize REITs or MLPs for Traditional or Roth IRAs.
- Rebalance annually to keep tax efficiency aligned with your investment goals.

Selecting the optimal account is often just as crucial as picking the right stock. In a traditional IRA or 401(k), dividends grow tax-deferred; taxes are paid on withdrawal, typically at a lower bracket in retirement. Roth IRAs offer tax-free growth and withdrawal. Taxable accounts, however, tax dividends each year — unless qualified and at a lower rate.

Account Type	Dividend Handling	Example Use Case
Traditional IRA	Tax deferred until withdrawal	Near-retiree lowering taxable income over time
Roth IRA	Tax-free growth and withdrawal	Early-career investor optimizing for long-term compound return
Taxable Account	Dividends taxed annually, at bracket rate	High-income individual with maxed-out retirement accounts

Mathematically, investing $10,000 in dividend stocks with a 4% qualified yield in a taxable account, taxed at 15%, grows to about $14,949 after 10 years. The same investment in a Roth IRA grows to $14,802 (similar, since taxes are avoided entirely). With ordinary dividends taxed at 24% over the same period, the taxable account reaches only about $14,332, showing the real impact of tax treatment over time.

For reinvestment, assessment criteria include:

- Your stage of life (accumulation vs. income)
- Immediate cash needs
- Growth vs. income priorities

Decision points:

- If you're early in your career, reinvesting dividends can maximize compounding.

- Approaching retirement, you may begin diverting dividends to cash for expenses.
- If you rely on investments for living expenses, regular dividend payouts make sense.

Implementation steps involve setting your brokerage for automatic dividend reinvestment (DRIP) or cash payout. Monitoring metrics include dividend yield growth, cash flow consistency, and total portfolio return.

For example, a 35-year-old reinvesting $2,000 in annual dividends at 4% sees that amount grow to about $29,601 in 30 years (with compounding). Taking dividends in cash yields just $60,000 collected over the period — showing the compounding's dramatic effect.

International investing adds a new layer of consideration. Countries like the U.K. often withhold 0-15% for U.S. investors; Canada withholds 15% with tax treaty benefits, while Switzerland withholds 35%, reduced to 15% via treaty. These rates can sometimes be reclaimed or minimized through proper paperwork (IRS Form W-8BEN for U.S. investors). Changes in currency can result in gains or losses, and broker fees for currency conversions should receive special attention. To avoid double taxation, use brokers that automatically apply tax treaty benefits and maintain clear records for foreign tax credits.

Practical tools are essential:

- Portfolio Tracker: Sharesight, Morningstar Portfolio Manager
- Tax Estimator: TurboTax TaxCaster, IRS Withholding Estimator
- Dividend Alert: Seeking Alpha, Simply Safe Dividends
- Account Aggregator: Personal Capital, Mint

Tool Type	Example	Main Function
Portfolio Tracker	Sharesight	Tracks portfolios, calculates returns, and income
Tax Calculation	TurboTax	Estimate the tax owed on dividends.
Dividend Alert	Seeking Alpha	Notifies of payouts/dividend changes
Aggregator	Personal Capital	Centralizes all financial accounts

A practical action plan for implementation:

1. Open the necessary accounts (Roth IRA, Traditional IRA, or brokerage).
2. Research and select your first stock, focusing on tax treatment and diversification.
3. Gather and store dividend records, 1099-DIV forms, and tax identification documentation.
4. Set up your portfolio monitor — choose a tracker, tax tool, and dividend alert system.

For your exercise:

- Add up last year's dividend income, classify it by type, and calculate hypothetical tax owed using current brackets.
- Choose accounts for each holding, weighing tax treatment and personal needs.
- Decide if you will automatically reinvest or take cash from each holding, justifying the choice based on your objectives.
- Establish recurring monthly or quarterly reviews using your chosen tracker and alert system.

Finally, use the downloadable Monthly Dividend Planner. This spreadsheet, integrated with your trackers, helps you plan for tax payments, schedules not-yet-received dividends, and provides a clear record for annual reporting. It ties together tax optimization, account selection, reinvestment, and monitoring — helping you maximize after-tax growth and maintain a steady dividend income stream.

Now that we understand the fundamentals of dividend investing and how to build a sustainable, long-term income portfolio — even without a financial background — we can confidently begin crafting our path to financial independence through the stock market. By selecting reliable dividend-paying stocks, leveraging reinvestment strategies such as DRIPs, and optimizing tax-efficient account choices, investors can generate predictable cash flow while harnessing the power of compounding growth over time. Equipped with practical tools and knowledge, aspiring entrepreneurs and professionals alike are well-positioned to take actionable steps toward creating diversified passive income streams that support lasting wealth and greater freedom beyond traditional employment.

FIVE
CRYPTOCURRENCY AND BLOCKCHAIN INCOME

Have you ever wondered how some people manage to earn money from cryptocurrency without constantly buying and selling? The world of digital assets is often seen as confusing and risky, especially for those new to blockchain technology. Questions about where income can come from, how much effort it takes, and what dangers might lie ahead often leave beginners unsure about taking the first step.

This chapter will explore various ways to generate passive income using cryptocurrencies. It will explain concepts like staking, yield farming, airdrops, and NFTs, showing how each method works and what you need to participate. At the same time, it will highlight important risks, such as market volatility and common scams, so you can approach opportunities with caution and confidence. By gaining a clear understanding of these options, you will be better prepared to responsibly build income streams within the blockchain ecosystem.

EARNING METHODS AND OPPORTUNITIES: STAKING, YIELD FARMING, AIRDROPS, AND NFTS

Staking allows investors to earn rewards by actively participating in the validation of blockchain transactions. On proof-of-stake networks, such as Ethereum and Cardano, users "stake" or lock up their tokens as collateral in order to validate transactions, maintain network security, and earn incentives. Ethereum requires a minimum of 32 ETH to run a solo validator node directly, with returns averaging 4–5% annually. However, pooled staking solutions like those offered by Lido or Rocket Pool permit participation with smaller amounts, as low as 0.01 ETH, while pooling assets with others. Cardano's staking is accessible through native wallets like Daedalus or Yoroi, with no strict minimum and annual rewards of approximately 4–6%. A typical staking process begins by installing the respective cryptocurrency's wallet, transferring tokens, selecting a staking pool, and delegating assets directly through the user-friendly interface. Most platforms clearly display available pools, expected yield, and fees. Beginners benefit from built-in tutorials, simple pool selection, and robust customer support. The main technical requirements include a secure wallet, a reliable internet connection, and basic familiarity with wallet operations. Staked tokens usually remain locked, meaning withdrawal is either restricted or possible only after a cooldown period.

Yield farming involves supplying digital assets to decentralized finance (DeFi) protocols in return for a share of the transaction fees or interest generated. Popular platforms such as Uniswap and Aave have streamlined tools for both liquidity provision and lending. On Uniswap, users deposit pairs of cryptocurrencies into "liquidity pools," enabling decentralized trading and earning a percentage of trading fees — typically around 0.3% of every trade proportional to their share of the pool. Aave enables users to lend assets directly, with interest rates for stablecoins like USDC or DAI often ranging from 3% to 8% APY depending on market conditions. Accessing these platforms requires connecting a Web3 wallet, such as MetaMask, to the protocol, choosing the asset or liquidity pool, and confirming the smart contract transaction. Uniswap's interface displays current liquidity, pool share, and estimated returns, while Aave provides clear APR metrics and risk scores for each asset. Minimum deposits range from a few dollars' worth of tokens on Uniswap to slightly higher for more niche assets. Most platforms operate via web browsers with straightforward dashboards, guides for deposit/withdrawal, and

24/7 digital support. The main time commitment comes from monitoring rewards, rebalancing positions, and adjusting to changing yield rates.

Airdrops serve as promotional rewards distributed by projects to active community members or early supporters. They help bootstrap user adoption and create incentives for engagement before or during a token launch. Historic examples include Uniswap's 2020 airdrop of 400 UNI tokens — worth around $3,000 at launch — to anyone who had used the platform before a certain date. Another well-known event is the dYdX airdrop, which distributed thousands of dollars' worth of tokens to traders and liquidity providers based on past usage. To qualify for airdrops, users must typically meet criteria such as holding specific assets, completing tasks, or participating in on-chain governance. Reliable platforms for tracking upcoming airdrops include CoinMarketCap's Airdrop calendar and Airdrops.io. Verifying an airdrop's authenticity requires checking official project channels, reviewing announcement details on Twitter or Discord, and avoiding requests for private keys or additional funds.

NFTs (non-fungible tokens) offer passive income opportunities beyond simple buying and selling. Creators can encode royalties, often set at 5–10%, directly into smart contracts, ensuring they automatically receive a percentage of future resale prices. On OpenSea, artists like Beeple and musicians such as 3LAU have fetched millions while earning continuous royalties from every subsequent sale. Other successful NFT projects include Decentraland (digital land), Bored Ape Yacht Club (collectibles), and Foundation (artwork). To mint and list NFTs, users create a digital wallet, connect it to a major platform (e.g., OpenSea or Rarible), and upload their digital asset. The interface guides the user through filling metadata fields, setting royalties, and paying a one-time transaction fee, called "gas." Most platforms support beginner-friendly workflows that include previewing your NFT and tracking royalties. Minimum costs are generally the required gas fees and occasionally a listing fee, which can range from a few dollars to over $100 when network traffic is high. Time investment centers on creation, listing, and occasional promotion. Strong customer support, fraud protection, and clear dashboards help newcomers manage their NFT income and sales effectively.

These methods increase in both complexity and income potential as investor familiarity and involvement deepen, preparing participants for greater opportunities and corresponding risks that follow.

RISK MANAGEMENT, SECURITY, AND PRACTICAL ACTIONS FOR CRYPTO INCOME

Before entering the world of cryptocurrency investing, understanding the basic risks and security requirements is a necessity. Cryptocurrency trades 24/7 and often operates without the regulatory oversight found in traditional finance, making asset protection a core responsibility for individual investors. Market participants face unique threats alongside the promise of high returns, and success starts with building a solid defensive approach.

The variety of scams and risks in the crypto space is striking. Rug pulls — where developers abandon projects and abscond with investors' funds — remain one of the most damaging. In 2021 alone, more than $2.8 billion was lost to rug pulls, with notorious examples like the Squid Game token wiping out millions within hours. Phishing attacks are widespread, targeting individuals through fake emails, direct messages on platforms like Discord or Telegram, and malicious websites that mimic legitimate crypto portals. If a user unknowingly enters their wallet information or seed phrase, their entire wallet can be drained within moments. Pump-and-dump schemes also prevail, particularly in lesser-known tokens, where small groups use social media hype to drive prices up before selling, leaving retail investors with worthless coins. These schemes often gain traction within Telegram groups or Reddit threads, using fake endorsements and fabricated price targets.

Crypto asset values can swing dramatically within short timeframes, which magnifies risk. For instance, during May 2021's market crash, Bitcoin dropped over 30% in a single day, and altcoins saw even deeper slides. Price volatility stems from factors including market speculation, regulatory news, and the influence of major holders known as whales. New investors are often surprised by how little it can take — a rumor, a tweet, or a hacker's declaration — to send prices soaring or crashing.

Red flags in crypto projects are tangible and can be systematically checked. Lack of publicly available white papers means an absence of technical vision or planning. Anonymous or unverified team members should immediately spark skepticism, as transparency is a key marker of legitimacy. Promises of guaranteed returns, rapid multiplication of investments, and suspiciously high staking rewards usually signal unsustainable models or outright scams. Avoid project websites that don't have a clear use case or are overflowing with poor content. Investors are urged to research extensively: reading through documentation, checking developers' history on platforms like GitHub, and examining audit reports from reputable firms.

Protecting digital assets relies on understanding where and how cryptocurrencies are stored. Hot wallets, such as MetaMask, are applications or browser extensions that keep private keys online, offering instant access for daily transactions and decentralized applications. MetaMask simplifies connecting to platforms like Uniswap or OpenSea, but its internet connection exposes it to phishing and malware threats.

For safer storage, cold wallets such as hardware devices — Ledger Nano X and Trezor Model T are industry leaders — keep private keys offline, out of reach from online threats. These tools act like digital safes; funds only leave when the user physically connects the device and confirms the transaction. Best practices for all wallets include storing seed phrases offline on paper, never sharing them or saving them in cloud storage, and enabling two-factor authentication via dedicated apps like Google Authenticator. Using unique, complex passwords and changing them regularly adds another layer of protection.

Long-term holding of trusted cryptocurrencies — commonly called HODLing — minimizes exposure to short-term volatility and speculative risks. Bitcoin (BTC) and Ethereum (ETH) are foundational assets due to their adoption and strong developer communities. Solana (SOL) and Cardano (ADA) present additional opportunities, with beginner-friendly ecosystems and active development. By holding rather than trading frequently, investors sidestep emotional mistakes like panic-selling during a dip or speculative buying on a spike, two actions known for decimating portfolios.

A first practical step is downloading MetaMask for hot storage (for interacting with DeFi platforms) and purchasing a Ledger device for storing significant assets long-term. When setting up these wallets, it is essential to record the seed phrase by hand and store it in a secure, offline location. Enabling device-level two-factor authentication and keeping wallet software updated reduces the attack surface further. For monitoring holdings and prices, tools like CoinGecko, Blockfolio, and Zerion offer tracking across multiple blockchains and wallets without exposing private keys. Portfolio tracking applications provide consolidated overviews, enabling smarter decisions.

Evaluating new projects requires a checklist approach. Confirm the legitimacy of the team by researching LinkedIn profiles or matching GitHub history. Examine tokenomics: check for unfair initial allocations or small circulating supply versus total supply. Review audit reports from established firms such as CertiK or Quantstamp. Assess the transparency and frequency of communication via official channels like Twitter, forums, and Discord. If any stage reveals inconsistencies or evasiveness, the risk is usually unjustifiable.

Investors who set up strong security defenses, manage risks methodically, and research thoroughly position themselves to explore the opportunities in crypto while safeguarding their assets against common and costly threats.

Now that we know the main ways to earn passive income with crypto — staking, yield farming, airdrops, and NFTs — and understand the need for careful risk management and security, new investors can more responsibly explore this changing field. By carefully researching these opportunities, putting in place strong protections, and having realistic expectations about ups and downs and possible scams, readers can confidently start to create a variety of income sources from blockchain. This foundational knowledge empowers entrepreneurs and side hustlers to take their first practical steps toward integrating crypto into a broader strategy for financial independence and long-term wealth creation.

SIX

RENTAL PROPERTIES AND REAL ESTATE CASH FLOW

Picture getting your first rental check and finding that it covers more than the mortgage — an extra monthly income without any work. For many aspiring investors, this moment represents the promise of financial freedom, yet the road to consistent cash flow can be confusing. Questions arise about whether to buy or lease, how to measure profitability, and how much time managing tenants and property upkeep will demand. With so many options and potential pitfalls, beginners often feel overwhelmed before even making their first move.

This chapter will take you through the essential concepts needed to understand rental properties as a source of passive income. You will learn how to evaluate different types of deals, calculate returns with simple financial metrics, and explore strategies that fit various budgets and goals. Additionally, it will guide you through methods of managing these investments efficiently, including ways to automate routine tasks and decide when professional help is worthwhile. The goal is to equip you with clear knowledge so you can approach rental property investing confidently — even if you are just starting out.

EVALUATING DEALS: BUYING VS LEASING AND CASH FLOW ANALYSIS

Rental property investing generally centers on two powerful approaches. The buy-and-hold strategy involves purchasing real estate to own and rent for the long term, benefiting from monthly rental income and value appreciation over years. Lease arbitrage, on the other hand, skips property ownership. Here, an investor signs a long-term lease and sublets the property, often on short-term rental platforms, keeping the difference between rental income and costs.

Buy-and-hold's clear advantages include long-term wealth, steady cash flow, the ability to leverage equity, and favorable tax benefits like depreciation. However, this approach ties up more cash, carries market risk, and faces tenant turnover or property damage. Returns often come from monthly cash flow — say, collecting $2,000 in rent on a property with $1,500 in expenses yields $500 monthly. Over years, appreciation can add significantly more to your net worth. Typical annual returns range from 8% to 15% or more, factoring in both income and appreciation.

Lease arbitrage's allure lies in lower upfront investment since no purchase is needed. Entry is easier — sublease a $1,400/month apartment, furnish it, then top $2,400/month from short-term bookings. Investors pocket the $1,000/month margin after costs. Risks here include landlord restrictions, changing short-term rental regulations, and high vacancy rates. Returns can be high in the short term, but ongoing management is demanding, and there's no equity or appreciation gain. Annualized returns based on cash invested can easily exceed 30%, though volatility is higher.

Accessing these investments starts with traditional financing — mortgages require 15-25% down for single-family rentals, so a $250,000 home might need a $50,000 down payment plus closing costs. Credit score, income, and reserve requirements apply. Creative avenues like seller financing let the buyer make payments directly to the seller, sometimes with less strict approval and lower down payments. Partnerships allow splitting costs and responsibilities — one partner brings cash, the other finds and manages the deal. Joint ventures or syndication structures allow pooling funds, reducing individual capital needed.

Alternative strategies for those with limited savings include house hacking (renting a multi-unit property and living in one unit, letting other tenants cover expenses) or co-signing lease arbitrage arrangements with minimal startup cash.

Successful rental investment requires grasping key financial metrics. The cap rate, or capitalization rate, measures return on investment, excluding financing. If a property costs $200,000 and generates a net income of $16,000 per year after expenses, then the cap rate is calculated as $16,000 divided by $200,000, which equals 8%. Cash-on-cash return considers financing — if you invest $40,000 (down payment and closing costs) and annual cash flow is $6,000, your cash-on-cash profit is $6,000 ÷ $40,000 = 15%. Gross rent multiplier (GRM) quickly compares properties — divide property price by annual rent. A $240,000 property that rents for $2,000/month ($24,000/year) has a GRM of 10; lower GRMs often signal better deals.

Common Rental Expenses Breakdown

Expense Category	Example Monthly Amount	Notes
Mortgage Payment	$1,050	Includes principal & interest.
Property Taxes	$220	Varies by location
Insurance	$80	Landlord policy
Property Management	$160	Usually 8% of rent
Maintenance Reserves	$100	For repairs and vacancies
Utilities	$100	If owner-paid
HOA/Other Fees	$55	If applicable
Total	**$1,765**	

Case Study 1: High-Cash-Flow Property

A duplex in Cleveland purchased for $150,000 rents for $2,200/month. Expenses include a $900 mortgage, $150 in taxes, $75 in insurance, $100 in management, and $125 in reserves/utilities ($1,350 total). Monthly cash flow: $2,200 - $1,350 = $850 ($10,200/year). When an investment of $37,500 is made, the cash-on-cash return is calculated as $10,200 divided by $37,500, resulting in 27.2%. Appreciation may be minimal, but cash flow is strong.

Case Study 2: Strong Appreciation Potential

A Phoenix home costs $400,000 and rents for $2,200/month. Total expenses run $1,950, for a slimmer $250 monthly cash flow ($3,000/year). With $80,000 down, cash-on-cash return is 3.75%. However, if property value grows 6% annually, the house is worth $424,000 after one year, adding $24,000 in unrealized gain. Combined with cash flow, total return for year one is $27,000 ÷ $80,000 = 33.75%.

Establishing passive income requires thoughtful system setup from the beginning. Investors automate rent collection, schedule reminders for maintenance, and set up accounting software like Stessa or AppFolio for bookkeeping. Virtual assistants handle communications, property managers oversee day-to-day operations, and contractors remain on call for repairs. Landlords create onboarding checklists for tenants, standardize screening, and use cloud-based document storage. A well-aligned team includes property managers, bookkeepers, legal advisors, and leasing agents — each ensuring the owner's time commitment stays low.

By linking acquisition strategies, financing, and detailed analysis with disciplined property management and automation, investors build solid pipelines for returns and continuous growth, no matter the market's direction.

MANAGING, AUTOMATING, AND SCALING RENTAL PROPERTY INCOME

Owning rental property can deliver steady passive income with the right management approach. Investors face a pivotal choice: self-managing or hiring a professional property manager. Self-managing cuts costs but increases time and responsibility. Owners oversee marketing, tenant screening, rent collection, maintenance, legal compliance, and financial reporting. Typical out-of-pocket costs include advertising ($100 per listing), background checks ($30 per applicant), and repairs. Investors often spend 4–8 hours per unit monthly handling tenant requests, bookkeeping, and problem-solving.

Professional property managers handle marketing, screening, lease agreements, rent collection, maintenance coordination, and regulatory compliance. Standard industry fees range from 8 to 12% of monthly rent. For a $2,000/month property, expect $160–$240 in management fees plus tenant placement or leasing fees (often equal to one month's rent). Managers often mark up maintenance charges by 10–20% and may add small annual fees for inspections and renewals. This structure reduces owner involvement to oversight and decision-making but cuts into monthly cash flow.

Management Approach	Avg Cost	Owner's Time (per unit/month)	Responsibilities
Self-Manage	$130–$400	4–8 hours	All
Professional PM	$200–$260+	<1 hour	Oversight only

Industry examples show property managers like Greystar or Mynd offering digital portals for owners and tenants. Basic service packages typically include rent collection, maintenance coordination, and financial reporting, with add-ons for eviction handling or 24/7 support.

Digital tools streamline self-management. Tenant screening platforms — like Avail and RentSpree — run criminal, credit, and eviction checks instantly. Users invite tenants to apply online, assess standardized reports, and avoid fair housing violations with uniform criteria. Online rent collection systems such as Apartments.com and PayRent automate reminders, deposits, and late fee enforcement. Funds transfer in 1–3 business days, and tenants use ACH, credit, or debit cards.

Maintenance software — like Buildium and AppFolio — organizes service requests and dispatches vendors. Tenants submit issues online, owners approve work, and the system tracks costs for accounting. Document management tools, such as Dropbox or DocuSign, centralize leases, renewals, and legal notices. Financial tracking apps, including Stessa and QuickBooks, sync with bank accounts, categorize expenses, and generate profit/loss statements for each property.

Short-term rental investors boost efficiency with targeted automation. Smart lock systems (e.g., August, Schlage Encode) enable remote guest access. Owners create temporary codes that expire after checkout, reducing key hand-offs and enhancing security. Dynamic pricing tools like PriceLabs and Beyond optimize nightly rates based on market trends, occupancy, and special events, increasing revenue. Booking calendars on Airbnb, Vrbo, and Booking.com synchronize with channel managers such as Hostfully, eliminating double-bookings and manual updates. Automated messaging tools (Hospitable, AirGMS) schedule check-in instructions, reminders, and responses to guest questions. Cleaning platforms (TurnoverBnB) notify service providers of new reservations, set schedules, and process payments, ensuring units are ready after each stay.

Rental property owners enjoy several tax benefits. Mortgage interest payments on investment properties are fully deductible each year. For instance, a $1,800/month payment on a $350,000 loan can yield over $10,000 in annual interest deductions. Depreciation deductions allow owners to offset rental income by dividing the property's purchase price (minus land value) by 27.5 years. A $330,000 property with $30,000 attributed to land creates a $10,909/year deduction. A 1031 exchange defers capital gains taxes by swapping one property for another. For example, selling a $400,000 rental and buying a $500,000 property avoids immediate taxable gains if IRS timelines and requirements are met. Operating expenses — repairs, property management fees, utilities, and insurance — reduce taxable income; detailed receipts and logs maximize deductions.

The BRRRR method lets investors rapidly expand their portfolios. The five steps are: buy undervalued property; rehab to increase value; rent to a qualified tenant; refinance based on improved appraisal; and repeat using freed-up equity. For example, an investor purchases a fixer-upper for $180,000 and puts $30,000 in repairs, raising the value to $260,000. Renting it for $2,200/month meets lender requirements. Refinancing at 75% loan-to-value nets a $195,000 loan. Subtracting the original loan and rehab recovers initial capital to invest again.

Key BRRRR Calculations

- After-Repair Value (ARV): Property's value post-renovation, validated by recent sales
- Rehab and closing costs must not exceed the difference between the purchase price and the after-repair value (ARV), after accounting for equity requirements.
- Cash-Out: New loan amount (typically 70–75% of ARV) minus payoff and costs equals available funds

Timelines average 4–7 months from purchase to refinance; delays can occur from lengthy rehabs or tenant placement. Risks include underestimated repairs, low appraisals, and high vacancy. Successful BRRRRs require conservative calculations, skilled contractors, and reliable tenants.

Rental income steadily pays down mortgages, increasing owner equity and net worth. For example, if a property generates $900/month in positive cash flow, the owner accumulates $54,000 over five years, along with equity from principal paydown and appreciation. Repeating this process with multiple properties multiplies returns and enables faster acquisitions using new cash-out refinances.

Choosing property management methods and using automation tools makes work easier, improves tenant happiness, and boosts passive income — through clear actions that investors can start right away.

Now that we understand the fundamentals of evaluating rental property deals, generating positive cash flow, and effectively managing or automating operations, aspiring investors are equipped to confidently build a strong foundation for passive income. By applying careful financial analysis, choosing suitable acquisition strategies, and leveraging technology or professional management, beginners can minimize risks and maximize returns. This knowledge paves the way for scaling a profitable rental business portfolio that steadily grows wealth and supports long-term financial independence, empowering readers to take actionable steps toward escaping traditional work constraints and creating lasting economic freedom.

SEVEN
REITS - REAL ESTATE INVESTING WITHOUT PROPERTY

Have you ever wanted to invest in real estate but felt overwhelmed by the thought of buying property, managing tenants, or dealing with maintenance issues? The idea of earning steady income from buildings and land is appealing, yet many hesitate because traditional property investment comes with its set of challenges and demands. For someone balancing a busy career or exploring ways to build passive income streams, owning physical real estate may seem out of reach or too time-consuming.

Real estate has long been considered a powerful way to generate wealth and secure financial freedom. However, the hands-on nature of property ownership can limit who benefits from this asset class. Many aspiring investors search for methods that allow them to participate in the real estate market without the complexities of direct ownership. This raises questions about how one can gain exposure to real estate's income and growth potential while maintaining flexibility and minimizing effort.

This chapter explores Real Estate Investment Trusts (REITs), investment vehicles designed to make real estate accessible, liquid, and beginner-friendly. It discusses the different types of REITs, how they function, and why they have become popular among those looking for stable dividend income without the headaches of managing physical properties. Additionally, it offers guidance on building diversified portfolios tailored to various risk tolerances and income goals. By understanding REITs, readers will find practical strategies to incorporate real estate into their passive income plans, moving closer to financial independence with a manageable and flexible approach.

UNDERSTANDING REITS AND THEIR TYPES

A Real Estate Investment Trust, commonly known as a REIT, is a company that owns, operates, or finances income-generating real estate. Unlike buying a single home or apartment, investing in a REIT lets a person own a small part of a much larger mix of properties. The properties can include office buildings, shopping malls, apartment complexes, hotels, and even hospitals. The main idea is similar to the way a mutual fund operates. works, except that instead of buying bonds or stocks, a REIT pools together money from many investors to invest in real estate.

REITs are unique because of a legal structure that requires them by law to pay out at least 90% of their taxable income each year as dividends to shareholders. This rule, set by the U.S. Congress in 1960, was intended to give ordinary people a way to benefit from real estate income without needing to buy actual property themselves. For example, if a REIT earns $10 million in taxable income in a year, it must distribute at least $9 million as dividends. This high payout requirement is one reason why REITs are attractive for people looking to earn passive income. Many REITs have dividend yields between 4% and 8% per year, meaning that investing $1,000 could generate $40–$80 in annual dividends, which is often higher than what is paid by traditional stocks.

There are three main forms of REITs, each working a little differently. Equity REITs are the most common. These own and manage real estate themselves, collecting rent from tenants and making money as the value of the properties goes up over time. For instance, a well-known equity REIT like Simon Property Group owns shopping centers and malls. Another example is AvalonBay Communities, which owns and manages thousands of apartment buildings across the United States. These companies earn most of their money from rent payments.

Mortgage REITs, or mREITs, do not own real estate directly. Instead, they own or buy mortgages and real estate loans. They make money by earning interest on these mortgages, rather than collecting rent. Annaly Capital Management is one of the largest mREITs and invests in home mortgage-backed securities. Because Mortgage REITs depend on interest rates and loan payments, their income can be more sensitive to changes in the economy.

Hybrid REITs combine both approaches. They own physical properties like an equity REIT and also invest in mortgages like a Mortgage REIT. Starwood Property Trust is a real-world example. By mixing both strategies, Hybrid REITs try to balance the benefits and risks of owning buildings and providing real estate financing.

Investors choose REITs for several important benefits. First, REITs are generally very liquid. Unlike apartments or commercial buildings, which can take months or years to sell, investors can buy or sell shares in publicly traded REITs instantly during market hours on a stock exchange, just like other stocks. For example, if an investor needs cash, they could sell $500 worth of REIT shares in seconds, while it would take much longer to sell a piece of real property.

REITs add diversification to an investment portfolio. Factors like company profits or interest rates affect stocks and bonds, but real estate often moves differently. In 2022, the average 20-year annualized return on U.S. Equity REITs was about 9.9%, which can offer a meaningful counterbalance to other assets. This diversification can help reduce overall risk.

Another strength is the low minimum investment required. While buying a single property could take a down payment of $20,000 or more, investors can start with REITs for as little as the price of one share, often under $100. Some platforms even offer fractional investing, making ownership even more accessible to new investors.

There are key differences between public and private REITs. Publicly traded REITs are listed on stock exchanges like the New York Stock Exchange or NASDAQ. This makes them easy to buy and sell, and their prices are updated every second while markets are open. They are subject to strict regulation by the Securities and Exchange Commission (SEC) and must report their financials regularly, making them more transparent. Anyone with a brokerage account can invest in public REITs.

Private REITs, by contrast, are not traded on public markets. They are usually available only to institutional investors or high-net-worth individuals. Private REITs tend to be less liquid, sometimes requiring years before an investor can sell their shares. They have fewer reporting requirements and are less strictly regulated, so investors may have less information about their operations. This makes private REITs potentially more volatile and risky, but occasionally they offer higher returns to compensate for these extra risks.

The variety of REIT types, public or private, and their different structures give investors many options to choose from, based on their risk tolerance, goals, and preferences for passive income generation.

BUILDING AND EVALUATING A DIVERSIFIED REIT PORTFOLIO

Portfolio Construction Method

Start by defining your "freedom number." This is the amount of passive income you plan to generate per month. Build your portfolio so projected dividends cover or exceed this target. Select your strategy based on risk tolerance, income needs, and time horizon. Use the following risk-based models as guides, all using a $100,000 starting capital:

Conservative Model: Income Focus

- **Sector Allocation:**
- Residential: 40%
- Healthcare: 25%

- Commercial/Office: 20%
- Data Centers/Infrastructure: 15%
- **Sample Holdings:**
- Vanguard Real Estate ETF (VNQ): 40%
- Welltower Inc. (WELL): 15%
- Realty Income (O): 15%
- Public Storage (PSA): 10%
- Digital Realty (DLR): 10%
- Prologis (PLD): 10%
- **Expected Yield:** 4-5.5%
- **Risk Level:** Low
- **Holding Period:** 5+ years
- **Rebalancing:** Every 12 months

Balanced Model: Moderate Growth and Income

- **Sector Allocation:**
- Residential: 30%
- Retail/Commercial: 30%
- Healthcare: 15%
- Data Centers/Infrastructure: 25%
- **Sample Holdings:**
- Schwab U.S. REIT ETF (SCHH): 30%
- Simon Property Group (SPG): 20%
- Prologis (PLD): 15%
- Equinix (EQIX): 15%
- Welltower (WELL): 10%
- Digital Realty (DLR): 10%
- **Expected Yield:** 3.5-4.5%
- **Risk Level:** Medium
- **Holding Period:** 3-5 years
- **Rebalancing:** Every 6 months

Aggressive Model: Growth Emphasis

- **Sector Allocation:**
- Data Centers/Infrastructure: 40%
- Industrial/Logistics: 25%
- Specialty (Cell Towers, Self-Storage): 20%
- Residential/Healthcare: 15%
- **Sample Holdings:**
- iShares Cohen & Steers REIT ETF (ICF): 30%
- American Tower (AMT): 25%
- Prologis (PLD): 20%
- CubeSmart (CUBE): 10%
- Invitation Homes (INVH): 10%
- Ventas Inc. (VTR): 5%
- **Expected Yield:** 2.5-3.5%
- **Risk Level:** High
- **Holding Period:** 5+ years
- **Rebalancing:** Every 4 months

Use dollar-cost averaging by investing a fixed amount monthly (for example, $1,000/month split among selections above). This smooths out price fluctuations and helps avoid market timing mistakes.

Monthly income portfolios prioritize high-dividend, stable REITs, while growth portfolios allocate more to sectors and REITs with historically stronger appreciation. Adjust allocation on your portfolio worksheet to see how changes affect projected monthly income versus total value growth.

Portfolio Model	Target Yield	Income Focus	Growth Focus	Recommended ETF
Conservative	4–5.5%	High	Low	VNQ, WELL, O
Balanced	3.5–4.5%	Medium	Medium	SCHH, SPG, DLR
Aggressive	2.5–3.5%	Low	High	ICF, AMT, PLD

REIT Evaluation Framework

Evaluate each candidate REIT with consistent, objective criteria. Prioritize total return (dividends + growth) as it relates to your freedom number.

Key Metrics to Track:

- **Funds From Operations (FFO):** Measures recurring cash flow. Choose REITs with rising or steady FFO per share.
- **Dividend Yield:** Annual dividend divided by current price; look for sustainable yields above the REIT sector average.
- **Payout Ratio:** Portion of FFO paid as dividends; 70–90% usually signals stability without limiting growth.

Sector Considerations:

- Residential and healthcare usually deliver steady income. Retail and industrial reflect economic cycles more strongly. Data centers and infrastructure offer growth but can be more volatile.

Sector	Typical Yield	Stability	Growth Potential
Residential	3–4%	High	Moderate
Retail/Commercial	4–6%	Medium	Variable
Healthcare	3.5–5%	High	Moderate
Data Centers	2–3.5%	Medium	High
Specialty	2–4%	Medium	High

Market Cycle Analysis:

Assess local and national real estate trends, vacancy rates, and whether rents are rising or falling. In expansion phases, growth REITs outperform. For late-cycle conditions, shift the portfolio towards sectors with long-term leases (healthcare, residential).

Comprehensive Tools and Frameworks:

- **REIT Scorecard:** Assign scores (1–5) for FFO growth, dividend safety, management quality, and sector risk.
- **Diversification Matrix:** Tally sector exposure to avoid overconcentration.
- **Income Calculator:** Multiply shares held by expected dividend per share to see monthly income.
- **Risk Checklist:** Review leverage (debt/equity), sector risk, and geographic diversification before finalizing allocations.

Case Studies

Investor Type	Sample Holdings	Allocation	Expected Annual Income	Growth Projection
Retiree	VNQ, WELL, O, PSA, DLR	40%/15%/15%/10%/10%/10%	$4,800 (4.8% yield)	Low
Professional	SCHH, SPG, PLD, EQIX, WELL, DLR	30%/20%/15%/15%/10%/10%	$4,100 (4.1% yield)	Moderate
Young Investor	ICF, AMT, PLD, CUBE, INVH, VTR	30%/25%/20%/10%/10%/5%	$2,800 (2.8% yield)	High

Calculate progress monthly to track how close you are to your freedom number. Rebalance allocations as needed, using your risk checklist and updated market data, to maintain the right mix and pursue financial independence efficiently.

Now that we have explored the fundamentals of Real Estate Investment Trusts and how to build a diversified portfolio tailored to different risk levels and income goals, readers are equipped to confidently incorporate REITs into their passive income strategies. By understanding the unique benefits of REITs — such as liquidity, dividend payouts, and exposure to various property sectors — aspiring investors can make informed choices that align with their personal financial freedom targets. With practical frameworks for evaluating and balancing REIT holdings, this knowledge serves as a strong foundation to steadily grow passive income, reduce reliance on traditional employment, and move closer to achieving long-term financial independence.

EIGHT
DROPSHIPPING AND E-COMMERCE AUTOMATION

Starting an online business without holding inventory has become an increasingly attractive option for many aspiring entrepreneurs. The idea of running a store that sells products without the need to stock or ship them personally offers a promise of flexibility and scalability. Yet, behind this appealing model lies a complex web of decisions — from choosing the right products to marketing effectively and automating operations — that can be overwhelming to navigate.

This chapter will guide readers through the essential steps of building such a business. It covers how to identify profitable products, establish an efficient online storefront, and implement automation tools that reduce manual work. Additionally, it explores strategies for scaling the business while maintaining smooth operations and delivering excellent customer service. By understanding these elements, readers can create a passive income stream through dropshipping and e-commerce with greater confidence and clarity.

FINDING PROFITABLE PRODUCTS AND BUILDING YOUR STORE

Choosing the right niche forms the backbone of any successful dropshipping venture. A profitable niche isn't just about what's trending — it's about solving real problems or addressing clear desires within a particular group. For example, instead of broadly selling "kitchen supplies," targeting "eco-friendly kitchen products for busy parents" reaches a more specific group who cares about both sustainability and convenience. Another focused niche might be "pet care solutions for apartment dwellers," recognizing the unique needs of people who want to care for pets in smaller, urban environments.

A strong niche typically meets several criteria, including a specific customer profile, a clear problem or desire, and space for unique value. Imagine someone who loves to hike but struggles to find minimalist, lightweight gear for quick day trips. If existing brands cater mostly to advanced adventures with heavy gear, there's an untapped market for simple, affordable solutions.

Market research is essential to discover and test these opportunities. Google Trends is a valuable starting point; searching "reusable produce bags" over time can reveal steady or rising interest, indicating growing consumer awareness. If searches jump during certain months, like before summer farmers' markets, it can signal a seasonal peak. Reviewing Amazon Best Sellers for related categories shows what's in demand right now. Exploring "Home & Kitchen" might reveal top-selling silicone bags for food storage. Analyze their reviews — do customers mention missing features or frustrations? These are opportunities to improve on existing offerings.

On TikTok, viral products often signal future trends. Searching for hashtags such as #EcoKitchen or #PetApartmentHacks uncovers what creators and audiences are buzzing about. If several videos highlighting collapsible water bowls for dogs gain hundreds of thousands of views, this points to strong engagement and shareability. AliExpress Hot Products can help spot emerging bestsellers. Filter categories, sort by order volume, and scan recent reviews to grasp real customer experiences and whether the interest is new or saturated.

After market research, use a consistent product validation process to filter high-potential ideas. Start with demand indicators: check Google search volume via free keyword tools, tally Amazon review counts, and track TikTok or Instagram likes and comments per product type. A threshold like 5,000 searches per month for "eco-friendly lunch bags" signals healthy curiosity.

Competition analysis comes next. Is the Amazon results page packed with nearly identical listings with thousands of reviews each? High saturation means higher advertising costs and tougher differentiation. Look for gaps, like only a few brands offering machine-washable or fully biodegradable materials.

Profit margin calculations are essential to avoid products that look good but barely earn anything. For example, let's say eco-lunch bags cost $4 per unit on AliExpress, including shipping, and average $18 on Amazon. After subtracting about 15% in Amazon fees ($2.70) and leaving a buffer for marketing ($2.00), there's roughly $9.30 left. This is over 50% gross margin, which is healthy for a dropshipping product.

Shipping times directly affect customer satisfaction. Use supplier dashboards that display estimated delivery to target regions. If most customers are in the U.S. and the supplier can only deliver in 25–40 days, the product is much harder to automate and maintain. Prefer suppliers with local warehouses or ePacket/express options, keeping shipping under two weeks if possible.

Quality matters for long-term viability. Order samples or look for detailed photo reviews showing the product in real use. If several users complain about leaks or rapid wear of the product, "eco-friendly lunch bags," reconsider or source alternative suppliers. Devoting attention to product presentation, packaging, and branding also helps set apart similar offers from your competition.

When exploring potential pitfalls, market saturation is a frequent challenge. Run simple counts: if a niche returns dozens of similar top sellers and every Google ad is packed with familiar names, reconsider or look for a tighter sub-niche. To avoid generic products, focus on bundle deals ("starter kits" with unique add-ons), partnerships with micro-influencers, or custom packaging with personal notes. Brand positioning can hinge on visual storytelling: "We help city dog lovers keep pets healthy in apartments with space-saving, eco-smart essentials."

Validating a product might look like this: researching collapsible pet water bowls, you see 15,000 monthly global searches, three Amazon sellers with fewer than 200 reviews, a $4.90 landed cost, and a $17–$19 customer price. Social media reveals high engagement rates, and supplier review photos show quality. Shipping from a U.S. warehouse is available, averaging 5–8 days. These factors suggest a viable product with healthy margins and differentiation space.

E-commerce platforms offer different strengths. Shopify is popular for its drag-and-drop site builder, integration with apps like Oberlo, and transparent monthly pricing. It's scalable but has fees for premium features. WooCommerce plugs into WordPress, boasts flexibility and low upfront costs, but demands more technical know-how. Wix and BigCommerce aim for beginners, with simple storefront editors but fewer automation tools. Each platform links to dropshipping apps for product import, automatic stock updates, order forwarding, and tracking notifications. Choosing a platform that easily connects these tools is crucial for minimizing manual work and creating a business that runs smoothly with little intervention — setting the stage for true automation.

AUTOMATING OPERATIONS AND SCALING YOUR BUSINESS

When a dropshipping operation is ready to scale, transforming day-to-day management into a largely hands-off process hinges on intentional automation and effective outsourcing. Store owners quickly realize that managing everything manually isn't sustainable as order volume rises. Instead, integrating smart automated systems will free up time, reduce errors, and enable strategic focus on growth.

The first layer is automating order fulfillment. Apps like Oberlo, DSers, and AutoDS connect directly with your e-commerce platform, syncing orders as they're placed. These tools automatically send order details to suppliers, track shipment status, update customers with tracking numbers, and flag inventory shortages in real time. For instance, a

Shopify store using DSers can set up rules to auto-route orders to the optimal supplier and instantly notify customers at each fulfillment stage. Store owners can set inventory alerts to prompt reordering or temporarily pause advertising for products running low.

Customer service, often a bottleneck in scaling, can be largely automated. Chatbots like Tidio or Gorgias answer common questions — shipping times, order status, return policies — instantly, 24/7. Automated email systems, set up within platforms like Klaviyo or Mailchimp, provide tailored responses to inquiries such as shipping updates, refund processes, or account support. A ticket management solution like Zendesk funnels messages from all channels and auto-assigns them based on category and urgency. For more complex queries, clearly defined protocols empower virtual assistants (VAs) to resolve issues efficiently. Building a guide on when to escalate, how to issue refunds, and template responses for frequent situations ensures consistent customer experiences even as the support team grows or shifts.

Standard Operating Procedures (SOPs) underpin systematization. Developing SOPs for each core area — product listing, order processing, customer communication, returns, and dispute resolution — removes ambiguity and speeds up onboarding. For product listings, a step-by-step document defines image requirements, keyword integration, category mapping, and pricing formulas. Order processing SOPs cover everything from verifying details, pushing requests to suppliers, confirming fulfillment in the backend, and escalating backorders. Create standardized scripts for customer support covering inquiries, complaints, and refunds. Returns and dispute SOPs should clarify timelines, evidence requirements, and refund approvals. Storing these guidelines in a shared drive and maintaining a log of updates lets new VAs quickly become effective contributors.

To accelerate revenue, paid advertising automation becomes essential. With Facebook Ads, create targeted campaigns using lookalike audiences from past customers, set daily budget caps, and use rules that pause underperforming ads automatically. A good benchmark is aiming for a Return on Ad Spend (ROAS) of at least 3.0. On Google

Shopping campaigns, group products by margin and set custom bidding strategies, leveraging automated bid adjustments. TikTok Ads benefit from creative A/B testing — run at least three video variants at a time, track click-through and conversion rates, then reallocate budget to top performers. Use tools like AdEspresso for managing cross-platform ad experiments and tracking ROAS in real time. Continuous split-testing of ad copy, creative, and audience targeting ensures money is spent where returns are highest.

Influencer marketing can be streamlined for scale. Start by filtering Instagram and TikTok micro-influencers whose audience matches your niche, using platforms like Influence.co or Upfluence. A successful outreach template might read: "Hi [Name], we love your content! We think your followers would enjoy our [product]. Would you be interested in a paid collaboration or affiliate opportunity?" Set up scalable commission structures, such as offering 10-15% per sale. Track influencer performance via unique promo codes and UTM links in Google Analytics or Refersion. Regularly review conversions per influencer to double down on top performers.

For sustained organic traffic, SEO automation delivers compounding gains. Optimize product titles, descriptions, and meta tags with high-intent keywords discovered using Ahrefs or SEMrush. Use consistent keyword research workflows — identify main terms via competitor analysis and expand with long-tails found through Google Suggest. Build content marketing around buyer guides, FAQs, and evergreen blog posts, scheduling releases with editorial calendars. Technical SEO, such as site speed optimization, structured data, and mobile responsiveness checks, can be monitored with plugins and Google Search Console.

Email marketing can run on autopilot while nurturing revenue. Abandoned cart recovery flows trigger a sequence of three emails urging completion, often recapturing 15-20% of lost sales — set these in Shopify, Klaviyo, or Omnisend. Post-purchase upsell sequences offer related products or incentives within a week of the initial order. A welcoming series introduces new subscribers, shares brand values, and highlights bestsellers over 5-7 short messages. Retention campaigns send personalized offers every few months based on browsing or purchase data.

Case in point, an apparel dropshipper implemented Klaviyo's prebuilt flows and recovered $15,000/month in abandoned carts while using Gorgias chatbots to cut live agent shifts by 40%. Across all systems, monitor key metrics — order error rates, average reply times, support ticket resolution, and ad ROI. Routinely map, test, and refine each workflow, doubling down on what delivers an efficient, profitable, hands-off business.

Now that you understand how to identify profitable products, build an automated dropshipping store, and scale operations through smart marketing and efficient outsourcing, you are well-equipped to create a passive income stream that requires minimal hands-on management. By focusing on targeted niches, validating product demand, leveraging e-commerce platforms, and embracing automation tools, you can move beyond traditional work constraints toward financial independence. The next step is to apply these strategies consistently, refine your systems over time, and expand your online business steadily — transforming initial efforts into sustainable, scalable income that supports your broader journey to freedom and wealth diversification.

NINE
CREATING AND MONETIZING A YOUTUBE CHANNEL

Starting a YouTube channel can feel overwhelming, especially when you don't know where to begin or worry about being on camera. Many aspiring creators struggle with uncertainty about which topics will attract viewers consistently and how to turn their efforts into lasting income. The challenge grows when trends change rapidly and content loses relevance quickly, leaving creators frustrated as their channels stall or fail to generate steady revenue.

For those who prefer to work behind the scenes or are new to video creation, building a channel that earns passive income might seem out of reach. Questions about choosing the right niche, producing videos that continue to draw attention over time, and finding effective ways to monetize can create doubt. It's easy to wonder how others succeed in this space while feeling stuck trying to get started without the pressure of constant content updates or expensive equipment.

This chapter addresses these concerns by guiding readers through the process of creating a YouTube channel focused on evergreen topics — subjects that maintain interest and search demand long after the videos are published. It explores how to identify niches with strong income potential, explains key monetization methods beyond just ads, and highlights strategies for using automation and outsourcing to manage growth smoothly. Whether you're camera-shy or just beginning your online journey, understanding these principles can open the door to developing a sustainable source of passive income on YouTube.

SELECTING HIGH-POTENTIAL NICHES AND PRODUCING EVERGREEN CONTENT

A passive-friendly YouTube niche centers on topics with enduring interest. Evergreen content never loses its relevance, staying valuable for months or years. Viewers search for these topics consistently, creating opportunities for ongoing ad revenue and low-effort automation. An ideal passive niche allows for prerecorded videos or content scheduled well in advance, without relying on fast-changing trends or news cycles.

Timeless topics include meditation, which appeals to those seeking relaxation or stress management year-round. Personal finance tutorials attract regular search traffic, as viewers always look to improve their budgeting, investing, and financial planning skills. Productivity advice — like time management techniques or organization systems — remains relevant, helping people achieve their goals in any season. Channels offering ambient content such as study music, white noise, and nature sounds enjoy a steady audience, as new viewers always seek these for work or rest. These examples maintain long-term utility, attracting viewers at all times and maximizing passive earning potential.

A systematic approach to niche selection helps filter for profitability and fit. The process begins with identifying personal expertise or authentic interest. Content creators who enjoy their subject have a better chance at consistency and avoiding burnout. For example, someone with experience in budgeting may find personal finance tutorials satisfying and impactful.

Analyzing market demand and competition follows. Using tools like TubeBuddy, creators enter potential keywords related to their topic, such as "budgeting for beginners." TubeBuddy displays search volume statistics and reveals if the keyword is in high demand. VidIQ assists by measuring competitiveness and also showing top-ranking videos in that topic. The ideal scenario is a niche with steady search volume and moderate competition. Highly saturated fields may be harder to penetrate without unique content or a fresh perspective, while topics with low search volume may not sustain ongoing income.

Income potential assessment is a critical filter. Creators measure this by checking metrics such as estimated ad rates and affiliate marketing possibilities. Categories like personal finance, tech, and productivity historically command high CPMs (cost per thousand impressions). For example, personal finance channels on YouTube regularly report CPMs ranging from $15 to $30, significantly higher than entertainment or lifestyle content, which may only offer $2 to $5 CPM. Affiliate marketing also plays a significant role; technology review channels can generate recurring commissions by linking to software or products in descriptions.

A table can help clarify:

Niche	Average CPM ($)	Affiliate Potential	Sponsorship Demand	Evergreen?
Personal Finance	15-30	High	High	Yes
Tech Reviews	8-20	High	High	Yes
Productivity Tips	5-15	Medium	Medium	Yes
Ambient Music/Sounds	1-10	Low	Low	Yes

Monthly search volumes help gauge audience size. For example, the term "guided meditation" averages 100,000–200,000 monthly global searches, while "investment for beginners" registers 30,000–60,000. A target search volume for a profitable evergreen topic is typically between 10,000 and 100,000 searches per month, depending on sub-niche specificity and competition.

KeywordTool.io extracts long-tail versions of high-performing keywords. Typing "budgeting" reveals phrases like "budgeting tips for students" or "budgeting with irregular income," which often face less competition but serve substantial, specific audiences. These variations help carve out unique positioning without sacrificing demand.

Audience engagement signals the viability of a passive niche. Channels with high like-to-view ratios, consistent comments, and positive community feedback are more likely to earn from sponsorships and digital product sales. Educational and finance channels routinely attract brand partnerships and premium online course creation opportunities. For example, finance-focused channels like Graham Stephan's — built on investing insights — leverage affiliate links to stock trading platforms and sponsored integrations, generating passive streams beyond AdSense.

Data illustrates ad revenue potential across niches. Personal finance channels emphasize long watch time per video, driving higher ad views and repeat engagement. Technology channels successfully feature affiliate links for recurring software subscriptions, offering income from both YouTube ads and third-party commissions. Productivity creators bundle digital planners or online courses, further boosting passive earnings. Even ambient channels utilize playlist automation, resulting in continuous advertisements.

A structured process solidifies decision-making:

1. List top interests and expertise areas.
2. Use TubeBuddy, VidIQ, and KeywordTool.io to gauge demand, competition, and keyword opportunities.
3. Research top channels in each niche, observing ad types, affiliate links, and sponsored segments.
4. Compare CPM rates, engagement patterns, and monetization diversity.
5. Select topics that align with personal strengths and the required passive infrastructure — evergreen themes, high CPM, repeat viewing, and automation potential.

By looking at real-life ways to earn passive income with lasting content, creators can see a process based on valuable topics, smart ways to make money, and content that can grow easily. Channels focused on personal finance, tech tutorials, and study music highlight the necessary blend of topic selection, optimization tools, and revenue streams, preparing for sustainable, hands-off growth.

MONETIZING, AUTOMATING, AND SCALING YOUR CHANNEL FOR LONG-TERM SUCCESS

A successful path to YouTube passive income brings several monetization streams together, each stacking onto the last for compounding results. To build a machine that runs almost on autopilot, it's vital to understand the biggest monetization avenues and how they interlock. Start by focusing on the YouTube Partner Program, expand into affiliate links and sponsorships, and set up systems for scaling through automation and outsourcing.

YouTube Partner Program: Foundation of YouTube Revenue

The YouTube Partner Program (YPP) is the formal entry point for ad revenue. You must have at least 1,000 subscribers and either 4,000 valid public watch hours in the past 12 months or 10 million Shorts views in the last 90 days. Meeting these thresholds unlocks ad placements on your videos.

Implementation Steps:

- Enable two-step verification and adhere to all YouTube monetization policies.
- Apply for YPP in YouTube Studio.
- Once approved, monetize videos during upload or for past content.

Earnings Range:

A channel with 100K subscribers and consistent uploads in tech or finance can see $3,000-$5,000+ a month from ads, depending on CPM (cost per thousand impressions), which typically ranges from $2 to $20.

Optimization Tips:

- Place ads after the first 60 seconds for longer videos to boost mid-roll revenue.
- Analyze demographic data; audiences in the US, Canada, and Australia raise CPM.
- Encourage viewers to sign up for YouTube Premium — your channel earns a percentage based on Premium viewers' watch time.

YouTube splits ad revenue 55/45 with creators. For YouTube Premium, revenue comes from a pool, distributed based on watch time, giving a slight boost to channels with longer average viewing durations.

Affiliate Marketing: Expanding Beyond Ads

Affiliate marketing lets you earn a commission when viewers purchase products through special links you share. This is powerful in niches like tech reviews, beauty, and home improvement.

Requirements:

- Program approval from networks such as Amazon Associates, ClickBank, or ShareASale.
- Disclosure compliance (clearly state affiliations in video descriptions).

Steps to Implement:

- Integrate product or offer mentions within relevant videos.
- Pin affiliate links at the top of the description and as a YouTube comment.
- Use trackable link shorteners to monitor clicks and conversions.

Earnings Range:

Commissions range from 1% (Amazon) up to 75%+ (digital products on ClickBank). For example, a finance channel with 50K monthly clicks on credit card affiliate links could earn $2,500 to $10,000+ monthly if 1-2% convert.

Optimization Advice:

- Use callouts and on-screen prompts to guide viewers to descriptions.
- Rotate offers and highlight limited-time deals.

Sponsorships: High-Ticket Monetization

Brand deals provide a more predictable, sizable revenue stream. Companies pay for video mentions, dedicated segments, or entire sponsored videos.

Key Steps:

- Create a media kit (channel stats, audience breakdown, engagement rates).
- Use this formula to estimate rates: $20-$40 per 1,000 views for mid-roll integrations; $100-$200 per 1,000 views for dedicated content.
- Outreach template:
- "Hello [Brand], I'm [Name], creator of [Channel]. I average [X] views per video and have an engaged audience in [Niche]. I'd love to partner with [Brand] for a sponsored segment to

introduce your [Product/Service]. Attached is my media kit for review."

Implementation:

- Track responses, follow up after 7 days, and negotiate deliverables.
- Use platforms like FameBit, Grapevine, or direct email outreach.

A beauty channel securing two $3,000 package deals per month (audience 75K subscribers, high engagement) can reliably add $6,000 to monthly revenue.

Automation and Outsourcing for Scale

Automation reduces repetitive workload and maintains channel consistency:

- **Templates:** Prebuilt video descriptions, affiliate disclaimers, and title formats.
- **Content Calendars:** Use tools like Trello or Notion to map upload dates, sponsorships, and social promo.
- **Scheduling:** Batch-record and upload using YouTube's scheduler or TubeBuddy's bulk processing.
- **Team Management:** Assign video editing, thumbnail design, and community management to freelancers.

Outsourcing Essentials

Role	Typical Budget Per Video	Platform Suggestions
Video Editor	$50-$150	Upwork, Fiverr
Thumbnail Designer	$10-$35	Fiverr, 99designs
Scriptwriter	$40-$120	Upwork, Scripted
Virtual Assistant	$7-$15/hr	OnlineJobs.ph, Upwork

- Set clear guidelines and samples.
- Incorporate weekly quality reviews and audience feedback.

Compounding Revenue and Metrics for Success

Revenue multiplies when ad earnings, affiliate commissions, and sponsorship deals overlap. For instance, the channel "BeatTheBush" began with ad revenue, incorporated Amazon and credit card affiliate links, and subsequently secured sponsorships, resulting in a compound monthly income increase from under $1,500 to over $8,000 over a period of two years. Track your metrics: Target a 10% MoM (month-over-month) revenue lift with each new monetization stream.

The YouTube Automation Starter Kit

The Automation Starter Kit contains customizable description templates, outreach email templates, content calendar formats, recommended outsourcing checklists, and links to must-have tools (TubeBuddy, YouTube Studio bulk actions, and scheduling apps). Download each copy for your channel and deploy immediately as you practice automation and scaling through the next exercises.

Now that we understand how to select high-potential, evergreen niches and apply proven monetization strategies like the YouTube Partner Program, affiliate marketing, and sponsorships, we can confidently build a YouTube channel that generates passive income with minimal ongoing effort. By leveraging smart automation and outsourcing, even beginners or those who are camera-shy can scale their channels efficiently while maintaining consistent quality and audience engagement. This foundation not only opens doors to sustainable, diversified revenue streams but also empowers aspiring entrepreneurs to move closer to financial independence and freedom from traditional work constraints.

TEN
SELLING ONLINE COURSES AND TEACHING WHAT YOU KNOW

Many people possess valuable skills or knowledge they wish to share but feel held back by the technical challenges of creating and selling online courses. The idea of building a digital product that earns income around the clock seems appealing, yet daunting questions arise: Where do I start? How do I find a topic that others want to learn? What if I'm not a professional teacher or tech expert? These uncertainties often prevent potential creators from taking the first step toward turning their expertise into a scalable source of passive income.

In reality, successful online courses are not about delivering endless information; they are about guiding learners through meaningful change. People don't pay for facts — they invest in clear transformations that improve their lives. Whether it's mastering a new skill, overcoming a personal challenge, or achieving a career goal, the demand lies in actionable, proven methods that produce real results. This chapter explores how to identify those transformations within your own experience and create course content that meets a genuine need. It also examines practical options for hosting and selling your course, showing how you can maintain control without needing advanced technical skills. By understanding these core principles, you can build an online course business that grows steadily while freeing you from the limitations of traditional work.

FINDING YOUR COURSE TOPIC AND CREATING EFFECTIVE CONTENT

Imagine a world where knowledge is free, but real change is rare. This is the starting point for creating profitable online courses: transformation is what people pay for, not just more information. Anyone can search for calorie charts or "tips to lose weight." They will pay, however, for a system that helps them shed 20 pounds while working full-time and looking after their kids. Information shows "what." Transformation delivers the "how" — with real, lasting results.

Understanding the Transformation Principle

Consider two scenarios. Someone searches online and finds hundreds of coding tutorials. Most are free. But a complete beginner craving a new career needs more than random videos. They need a step-by-step programming roadmap, showing exactly how to go from no experience to landing a first tech job, with milestones, templates, and feedback. Similarly, while anyone can download a generic meal plan, a course that guides busy parents to create sustainable meal prepping habits while balancing work and children is much more valuable. It solves a more profound problem.

This is the transformation principle: successful courses create clear before-and-after results for learners. The question to ask is not, "What facts do I know?" but, "Where have I created meaningful change in my life or someone else's — and how can I walk others through the same journey?"

Problem-Solution Matrix Exercise

Unlocking your profitable course idea starts with drawing from your wins and challenges. The following framework makes the process practical and focused.

Step 1: List Personal Victories and Challenges Overcome

Begin by reflecting on your experiences. Jot down moments where you faced a challenge and came out on the other side stronger or more skilled. These can relate to work, health, money, relationships, or personal skills.

- Instruction: Write 5-10 experiences where you solved a problem or improved your situation.
- Example entries:
  - Changed careers from nursing to project management
  - Lost 30 pounds through home workouts
  - Learned conversational Spanish in six months
  - Paid off $20,000 in debt
  - Organized a cluttered home office for better productivity
- Validation criteria: The challenge must be common and relatable to others, not just a unique situation.

Step 2: Identify the Transformation Achieved

Now, for each entry, clarify the change that actually took place. What did your "before" look like compared to your "after"?

- Instruction: Describe the starting point and the outcome.
- Example entries:
  - From: Uncertain and burned out in healthcare To: Confident and happy in a new tech role
  - From: Overweight and low energy To: Fit, energetic, and running 5k races
  - From: Daunted by debt To: Debt-free and saving for a home
- Validation criteria: You should be able to express the benefit in clear, plain language.

Step 3: Define the Before and After States

Transformations are most compelling when the contrasts are direct and vivid. Document how life looked "before" and "after" for each achievement.

- Instruction: Use bullet points to draw a line between the before and after.
- Example entries:

Before	After
Disorganized workspace	Calm, productive office space
Struggling to lead team	Confident, effective manager
Confused about budgeting	Consistently saving money

- Validation criteria: The "after" must be a problem others desire to solve.

Step 4: Outline the Specific Steps Taken

Pay attention to the exact path you followed. People pay for a process that helps them move forward, milestone by milestone.

- Instruction: List the actionable steps you took for each transformation.
- Example entries:
    - Career change: Researched new industries, took online certification, networked with professionals, updated résumé, prepared for interviews
    - Health: Created a workout schedule, meal prepped Sundays, tracked meals, set weekly goals
    - Financial: Listed all debts, created a payment plan, cut unnecessary spending, set up automatic savings

- Validation criteria: Each step should be teachable, repeatable, and lead to tangible progress.

Proving People Want Your Solution

Finding a transformation is only part of the process. To ensure your course will sell, see if people are already searching for help. Search for similar courses on Udemy or other platforms; count reviews and see what people praise or complain about. Read comment sections for frustrations or results students still want. Browse Reddit threads in relevant forums to spot recurring obstacles, and join Facebook groups to observe questions that come up again and again. Make note of frustrations that are repeated. The more you see a specific problem mentioned, the greater the demand for a proven solution.

Courses that create real results — whether it's becoming a first-time manager, learning a new language, building better habits, or simply organizing chaos — are the ones people trust with their money. If you can define a transformation based on your own experience, showing exactly how you achieved it and proving others crave the same outcome, you've already built the foundation for a profitable course. The technical steps for building a course platform are next, and anyone can master them with the right tools.

LAUNCHING, SELLING, AND SCALING YOUR COURSE ONLINE

Deciding where to host your online course is the first step in turning your knowledge into steady income. Two main types of platforms are available: course marketplaces and self-hosted platforms. Each comes with its own pros and cons, shaped by cost, technical needs, and how much control you want.

Platform Analysis

Course Marketplaces

Platforms like Udemy or Skillshare make it easy to start. They handle all the tech, process payments, and bring in traffic from their user base. The setup is typically quick, requiring only uploads of your course material. This works well for creators who want to focus on content instead of promotion. However, marketplaces often keep 50-75% of each sale as commission, so your earnings per student drop. For example, an Excel mastery course priced at $49 might earn you only $12 to $15 after fees. Marketplaces have wide exposure, but you give up control over your pricing and student information. Ongoing updates are limited, and engagement features, except for basic Q&A or community spaces, are minimal. Most courses in marketplaces sell for $20-$100, with average conversion rates around 2-4% on platform traffic. Maintenance is low, but repeat sales can be challenging unless you continually create new courses.

Self-Hosted Platforms

Sites like Teachable or Kajabi give full control over sales, branding, and pricing. You keep most of your revenue, paying only for the platform or a small transaction fee (often $30-$150/month, with some transaction fees at 2-5%). You set course prices — maybe $297 for a social media marketing program or package a painting course for $97 plus monthly membership. Self-hosting brings ownership advantages: access to student emails, better engagement tools like live chat, quizzes, or certificates, and the flexibility to link with other software. However, you're also in charge of driving traffic, which means setting up payment gateways, emails, and integrations on your own. Setup typically takes 15-30 hours. The revenue potential is higher, and average conversion rates from your own audience reach 5–8%. Ongoing updates, tech maintenance, and marketing are your responsibility.

Platform Type	Setup Time	Pricing Range	Average Commission	Control over pricing.	Typical Maintenance
Marketplace	2-5 hrs	$20-$100	50-75%	Low	Low
Self-Hosted	15-30 hrs	$97-$997+	0-5%	High	High

Revenue and Control Examples

A watercolor artist sold 800 units of a $97 painting course on Udemy in a year, but after commissions, they received roughly $9,600. Another ran the same course through Teachable, sold only 300 units, but kept 95% of each sale — netting around $27,600. A premium coaching course for careers at $1,297 hosted on Kajabi, with a 2% sales page conversion and 4,000 targeted visitors per year, can generate over $100,000, especially with a single live onboarding webinar and group access. In all cases, control over content and student data translates into better upsell capacity and recurring revenue from memberships or bundles.

Building an Automated Sales Funnel

Lead Magnet Creation

For an Excel course, offer a downloadable "Top 10 Excel Formulas" guide. Watercolor example: a free video tutorial on creating vibrant washes. Social media marketing: checklist for winning your first 100 followers. These should be immediately useful, relevant, and quick to access. Expect opt-in conversion rates of 20-40% on targeted landing page traffic.

Email Sequence Structure

Automate a simple five-to-seven email nurture sequence.

1. Welcome and deliver lead magnet
2. Story and credibility (case study or personal results)
3. Common mistakes in the field

4. Value lesson: quick win or tip
5. Invitation to webinar or mini-course
6. Overcome objections / FAQs
7. Direct sales offer with time-limited bonus

Open rates typically start at 35-45%, with 2-5% purchase rates from engaged subscribers. Setup and integration using platforms like ConvertKit take about 2–4 hours.

Webinar Framework

Host a 60-minute live or automated webinar, blending teaching with storytelling and soft selling. Use a clear agenda:

- 10 min: Introduction and personal results
- 20 min: High-value teaching
- 10 min: Mistake busting and opportunities
- 10 min: Demo of your system
- 10 min: Offer and Q&A

Webinar conversions run 6-10% if traffic is warm (from your email list).

Upsells and Integrations

After purchase, offer personal coaching, a membership, or bundled classes. Set up integrations to automatically enroll students, tag them for follow-up, and unlock bonuses. Platforms like Zapier help automate these steps.

Sustainable Revenue Models

Mix entry courses ($27-97) for wide reach, mid-tier ($197-497) for signature content, and premium ($997+) with coaching or group sessions. Bundling related classes increases transaction value by 30-50%. Add membership options for ongoing access ($29-49 / month), and offer affiliate deals (20-30% commission) to expand reach.

Practical Exercise

- List your must-have platform features (commission, maintenance, engagement tools)
- Sketch out your lead magnet and email sequence for your topic
- Choose three price points for your offers
- Outline the automation steps, noting key integrations

The right decisions help turn your course into a true business asset that runs — and grows — on autopilot.

Now that we understand how to identify a compelling transformation based on our own experience and validate its demand, we can confidently create online courses that deliver real, lasting results to learners. By choosing the right platform — whether a marketplace for ease or self-hosting for greater control — and building automated sales funnels with lead magnets, email sequences, and webinars, we set the stage for scalable passive income. With thoughtful pricing strategies and ongoing engagement through upsells and memberships, turning knowledge into a sustainable business becomes not only achievable but also rewarding. This foundation empowers aspiring entrepreneurs and professionals to move beyond traditional limits and build diversified income streams with lasting impact.

ELEVEN
PROFITING FROM DIGITAL PRODUCTS AND TEMPLATES

Have you ever wondered how some entrepreneurs build thriving businesses by selling digital products that require little ongoing effort? Many begin with a simple idea — a planner, a template, or a checklist — and turn it into a reliable income stream that grows far beyond their initial investment of time. Yet for most people, knowing where to start or how to navigate crowded online marketplaces can feel overwhelming. Questions about designing appealing products, choosing the right sales platform, and reaching potential customers often stand in the way of turning ideas into profit.

This chapter will guide you through the process of developing digital products from scratch using accessible tools and efficient workflows. You'll learn how to identify market needs, design valuable offerings, and choose the best platforms to reach your audience. We'll also explore strategies for building visibility and engaging customers through email marketing, helping you grow your sales steadily while maintaining quality and brand consistency. By mastering these steps, you can create scalable digital assets that play a lasting role in your financial independence.

FROM IDEA TO CREATION: BUILDING PROFITABLE DIGITAL PRODUCTS EFFICIENTLY

Digital products are thriving due to their scalability and ease of distribution. Among the most in-demand categories, planners, templates, and printables consistently rank at the top of bestseller lists. For example, a "Social Media Content Calendar" template targets freelance marketers who struggle with consistent posting. This product can typically be created in under four hours utilizing a beginner's understanding of Google Sheets or Canva. Social media agencies and solo entrepreneurs are willing to pay $12–$25 for a ready-to-use, customizable calendar. Market demand is high, indicated by thousands of sales and positive reviews for similar items on platforms like Etsy, where related keywords show steady search volume month to month.

A "Wedding Planning Checklist" printable addresses overwhelm and forgotten details for engaged couples, especially those managing large events on their own. This printable may take two to six hours to develop using Canva or PowerPoint, requiring basic graphic and organizational skills. The typical price point is $10–$15, with high customer interest seen in recurring Etsy and Creative Market bestsellers. Customers praise checklists that break down the process into timelines and vendors, flagging "easy-to-follow" and "comprehensive" as desirable features.

Personal finance is another profitable niche, exemplified by a "Personal Budget Tracker" in Google Sheets with automated formula calculations, pie charts, and customizable monthly tabs. It solves the challenge of tracking expenses and sticking to savings goals — frequent pain points for recent graduates and young families. While more detailed than a printable, it can be developed in four to eight hours with intermediate spreadsheet skills. Price points range from $8 for basic versions to $40 for complex trackers with dashboards and tutorials. Consistent top-seller status and requests for new features in user reviews attest to high market demand.

To identify winning product ideas, research real customer behavior and competitor offerings. Start by browsing the top charts on Etsy and Creative Market. Record how often products appear, their review counts, and sales estimates where available. For deeper insight, sift through the customer reviews section and note recurring requests (such as "please add a yearly overview") or complaints ("the formulas are wrong in the March tab"). Pinterest is also a rich source for trending topics; search niche-specific terms (like "teacher lesson plan printables") and observe which pins have high engagement statistics.

Seek product gaps by comparing the features of current bestsellers with what reviews request. If dozens appreciate a meal planner but mention it's undated, this signals an opportunity to release a version with date selectors or themed variants (for example, a 12-week meal planner with weekly grocery lists, macro tracking, and links to healthy recipes).

Market Research Activity

- Select three popular products in your chosen niche.
- Create a table listing each one's features, price, and review highlights.

Product Name	Features	Price	Review Highlights
Weekly Fitness Log	Habit tracker, progress graphs	$14	"Easy to update," "Colorful"
90-Day Meal Planner	Recipe database, grocery lists	$17	"Wish it had calorie tracker"
Home Budget Sheet	Income/expense auto calc	$22	"Formulas work perfectly"

- Note three improvements you could make, such as adding color themes, integrating printable and digital formats, or including detailed user instructions.

- Outline your potential unique selling points, like "custom calorie tracking for meal plans," "auto-updating holiday budgets," or "print and digital bundle."

With product ideas validated, accessible design tools streamline creation. Canva's grid system enables clean, balanced layouts for planners and checklists, while drag-and-drop elements reduce the learning curve. Google Sheets supports complex logic with built-in formulas, making it easy to automate calculations for budget and habit trackers. PowerPoint allows batch creation of printable pages, using master slides to ensure consistency.

A step-by-step workflow supports efficient product development:

1. Validate your concept with marketplace feedback and competitor comparisons.
2. Plan the layout, using rough sketches or digital mockups on Canva.
3. Build out core content — fill in checklist steps, calendar dates, or tracker fields.
4. Select visuals such as icons, fonts, and color schemes.
5. Optimize format for print and digital delivery: test layouts for both PDF and editable files.
6. Perform quality checks such as proofreading, formula validations, and user flow reviews.

Reduce workload by outsourcing tasks like proofreading to freelancers on Upwork or hiring a graphic designer from Fiverr for custom illustrations. AI text generators like Jasper can assist with instructional content or guided prompts. Virtual assistants are available through platforms such as Belay and OnlineJobs.ph for repetitive formatting tasks. Batch produce product variations by duplicating templates and adjusting details — creating a suite of budget planners for students, families, and freelancers in one session.

The Digital Product Launch Toolkit includes step-by-step layout planners, editable style guides, and usage instruction sheets. Use the layout planner for arranging each product's sections logically. Style guides set fonts, color schemes, and brand elements for a cohesive look. Instruction sheets walk buyers through first use and common troubleshooting issues, increasing customer satisfaction and reducing support queries.

Conclude this section by choosing one researched product and using the provided planner template to design your first draft. Refine your product with the quality benchmarks outlined above, ensuring all formulas work and instructions are clear. With a completed draft in hand, you'll be ready to select the ideal marketplace and build launch momentum using email marketing, covered in the next section.

SELLING AND SCALING: PLATFORMS, VISIBILITY, AND EMAIL MARKETING FOR LASTING SUCCESS

When choosing a platform for your digital product, align your selection with your product type and long-term goals. Etsy is a strong fit for printables, digital art, and design templates — products with strong visual appeal and broad consumer interest. Gumroad attracts creators selling e-books, audio files, courses, and memberships, offering flexible pay-what-you-want pricing and robust creator communities. Payhip stands out for its simplicity and global reach, ideal for new sellers testing different digital asset types, from software to fitness plans.

Etsy deducts a 6.5% transaction fee from each sale, a 3% + $0.25 payment processing fee, and charges $0.20 per product listing. Payouts are usually made within 2–3 business days after a sale, making cash flow management predictable. Gumroad charges 10% on free accounts and 3.5% + 30¢ for paid accounts ($10/month for Pro users). Payouts via PayPal or direct deposit occur every Friday, with a two-day buffer for payment processing. Payhip strikes a balance with a 5% transaction fee on the free plan, 2% on Plus ($29/month), and 0% on Pro ($99/month), with payments processed instantly via Stripe or PayPal.

Each marketplace presents unique advantages. Etsy's mature built-in audience means instant exposure, with over 90 million active buyers reported annually, though competition can be fierce and keyword optimization critical. Gumroad supports large file uploads (up to 16GB), lets you set multiple price points, and facilitates EU VAT collection at no extra cost. However, it may not bring significant organic traffic; you'll need to drive most customers yourself. Payhip offers clean, simple storefronts, strong customization, and built-in affiliate management, but its organic traffic is lower than Etsy's ecosystem, so off-site promotion is vital.

Marketplace	Monthly Fees	Transaction Fees	Payment Processing	Features	Tech Requirements
Etsy	None	6.5% + 3%+$0.25	2–3 days	Built-in traffic, reviews, SEO tools	None (easy onboarding)
Gumroad	$0/$10	10%/$0	Every Friday	Subscriptions, analytics, VAT	Minimal (basic account setup)
Payhip	$0/$29/$99	5%/2%/0%	Instant	Customization, affiliate, memberships	Basic (easy to moderate)

To boost product visibility, leverage keyword optimization by analyzing competitor listings and high-traffic search terms using tools like Marmalead (for Etsy) or Google Trends. Place relevant primary keywords in your product title, description, and tags. An example of an optimized Etsy title: "Minimalist Budget Planner PDF – Printable Finance Tracker, A4 & Letter Size, Instant Download." Incorporate keywords naturally in your description — avoid stuffing.

Pinterest marketing is powerful, especially for visually oriented products. Create high-quality, vertical pins (1000x1500 px), adding keyword-rich descriptions. Pin consistently (at least 5 pins per week) to relevant boards, and join group boards in your niche for expanded reach. Pins with clear calls-to-action ("Download now," "Save for later") convert more browsers into buyers. Top-performing pins can drive 30–50% of total shop traffic.

Lead magnets like free digital samples, checklists, or mini-guides can capture potential buyers' emails and spark interest. Use Payhip's built-in free download feature or Gumroad's $0+ pay-what-you-want pricing as entry points, allowing customers to access your lead magnet in exchange for their email.

Traffic generation should combine organic social sharing, content marketing (e.g., publishing tutorials featuring your product), and paid ads if budget allows. Sharing customer reviews and use-case photos boosts credibility, nudging skeptical visitors toward purchase.

A robust email list enables direct customer engagement. Start by integrating opt-in forms on every product page and confirming new signups through a welcome email sequence:

- Email 1: "Welcome + your free planner download"
- Email 2: "How to get the most out of your digital planner" (with product tips)
- Email 3: "Exclusive 15% discount on your next purchase"

During product launches, send teaser emails ("Coming soon: The Ultimate Productivity Bundle") followed by a launch announcement, a benefits-focused reminder, and a last-chance scarcity message ("Sale ends in 6 hours!"). After purchase, nurture loyalty with surprise discounts or access to a VIP club. Automating sequences via ConvertKit or MailerLite saves time.

Branding is important in all marketplaces. Specializing in a niche — such as "planners for teachers" or "watercolor clipart sets" — lets you position yourself as the go-to expert, making your brand memorable. Consistent visuals, voice, and product presentation across Etsy, Gumroad, and Payhip reinforce recognition. Use a professional logo, standardized listing photos, and customer-focused copy. Craft a brand statement, such as "Empowering productivity with beautiful, easy-to-use digital tools for educators worldwide."

For standout product listings, include a gallery of lifestyle images, a demonstration video (if the platform supports it), and clear download instructions. For example, the "Student Planner Bundle" with screenshots, testimonials, and a usage tutorial led to a 22% higher conversion rate compared to text-only listings.

By following these steps and using platform metrics to monitor your progress, you steadily improve sales outcomes and build a loyal customer base.

Now that you have a clear, step-by-step understanding of how to create, launch, and sell scalable digital products using accessible tools and effective marketing strategies, you are well-equipped to turn your ideas into profitable offerings. By carefully researching market demand, leveraging user-friendly design platforms, and selecting the right online marketplaces, you can build products that meet real customer needs while minimizing effort. Coupled with strong email marketing and consistent branding, these practices lay the foundation for growing a sustainable digital business. With this knowledge in hand, you are ready to take deliberate action toward financial independence by expanding your passive income streams through digital products and online sales.

TWELVE
STACKING YOUR INCOME STREAMS AND SCALING UP

Imagine juggling several tasks at once — each demanding attention, yet none quite thriving because your focus is scattered. Many aspiring entrepreneurs and side hustlers find themselves overwhelmed trying to manage multiple income sources simultaneously, only to see limited progress and mounting frustration. The challenge lies not in creating streams of passive income but in strategically combining and managing them to build lasting wealth without burning out or losing sight of priorities.

This chapter explores how deliberate selection and careful management of income streams can transform extra earnings into a sustainable financial foundation. It discusses practical ways to use time efficiently, reinvest profits wisely, and establish systems that grow and scale over time. By understanding these principles, readers will be equipped to build a diversified portfolio of income sources that work together smoothly, enabling them to move steadily toward financial independence with clarity and control.

COMBINING AND MANAGING MULTIPLE INCOME STREAMS: STRATEGIES AND PRODUCTIVITY METHODS

Building sustainable wealth through multiple passive income streams requires a disciplined, step-by-step approach that balances ambition with practical workflow strategies. The journey always begins with deep mastery of one or two streams before expansion. When an author wants to develop lasting income, the smartest path is to focus on one area — a well-crafted eBook, for example — until royalties flow consistently and the production process feels routine. Only then should the author consider branching into audiobooks, leveraging the same manuscript and their understanding of audience preferences, or producing online courses based on the book's subject. This incremental mastery cements the workflow, prevents overwhelm, and sets the foundation for stacking new streams later on.

Smart Selection of Complementary Streams

Compatibility plays a central role when adding new income sources. Synergies amplify returns while reducing redundant effort. A real estate investor who manages rental properties often expands into Real Estate Investment Trusts (REITs). The cash flow from rentals provides hands-on experience and insight, while REITs offer a hands-off, liquid alternative. Earnings from rentals can be partially reinvested into REITs, smoothing monthly returns. Similarly, a digital content creator might begin with a successful blog. Once the blog earns $500+ per month in ad revenue, the creator can repurpose popular articles into scripts for a podcast or YouTube channel, both targeting overlapping but unique audiences.

Here's how compatible streams naturally align to form an efficient workflow:

Core Stream	Add-On Stream 1	Add-On Stream 2
eBook author	Audiobook narration	Online video course
Rental property owner	REIT investments	Property management tools
Blogger	Podcast episodes	Social media mini-guides

The table underscores how each new stream leverages the audience, content, or cash flow of the core stream.

Complementary Workflows in Action

Once comfortable with primary income streams, entrepreneurs should turn individual assets into multiple products. Take a blog post about personal finance. The creator can record a podcast episode expanding on its points, then film a short YouTube video explainer, and extract quotes and tips for Instagram and Twitter. This four-pronged output requires very little new research or ideation; each variant reaches different user demographics.

A practical scenario unfolds like this:

1. Write a detailed blog post (2,000 words)
2. Record a 15-minute podcast using the blog as a script
3. Shoot a 5-minute video highlighting the post's most actionable tips
4. Draft five social media graphics summarizing key points

With proper planning, this sequence takes no more than 10–12 hours to complete. If each channel earns at least $50 monthly in ad revenue or affiliate commissions, the combined output delivers $200 per month for work done largely upfront.

The 80/20 Rule for Expansion Decisions

Selective focus magnifies results. The 80/20 rule suggests that roughly 80% of revenue comes from 20% of efforts. Identify what to prioritize by tracking actual returns. If an author tracks book royalties, they might see that one title earns $1,000/month, while three others make only $150 each. Rather than launch more books blindly, the author analyzes why the top title performs so well — genre, promotion channel, or audience. The goal: double down on similar high-performers by investing time in proven winners or by adapting their format (e.g., creating a workbook version).

Metrics clarify decisions. Set a threshold: only pursue new ventures projected to generate at least $100/month after three months. Content creator Pat Flynn, for example, grew his passive income by focusing on podcast episodes that consistently pulled in 70% of his sponsorship revenue, cutting projects that lagged behind.

Pitfalls, Solutions, and Work-Life Harmony

Common pitfalls include burnout, overcommitment, and poor tracking. Entrepreneurs often launch too many streams at once, diluting energy and seeing stagnant results. An actionable solution is to schedule "focus sprints" — two-month periods concentrated on a single new stream while maintaining the others.

Use simple project management tools. Trello helps writers and investors track progress. Content calendars — even just a shared Google Sheet — ensure deadlines and publishing cadences remain public and actionable.

Set time boundaries. Limit deep work to three 90-minute sessions per week for new stream development. Use metrics like weekly revenue and hours invested to assess whether to continue or pivot.

Systematic Workflow and Scalability

Efficiency and scalability rely on well-documented, repeatable processes. Templates for blog posts, podcast scripts, or landlord checklists help to automate future output. Business planning apps or simple SOPs ensure that each new addition fits with, rather than overloads, the existing system. These structures make adding streams feel like puzzle pieces snapping together, rather than jigsaw chaos. Productivity and time management become not just helpful but essential as each income stream multiplies. A systematic approach is the cornerstone of building resilient, scalable passive income.

SCALING UP: REINVESTING PROFITS, BUILDING SYSTEMS, AND PLANNING FOR FINANCIAL INDEPENDENCE

Analyzing the journey from a single passive income stream to a robust wealth-generating system demands a strategic approach to reinvestment, expansion, and optimization. Begin by earmarking 50% of net profits each month for reinvestment. Divide this allocation into two main buckets: 30% into low-cost index funds and 20% into Real Estate Investment Trusts (REITs), leveraging platforms like Vanguard (for index funds) and Fundrise (for REITs). Reserve another 20% for business growth tools such as ConvertKit for email marketing and Zapier for workflow automation. This structure creates a flywheel that builds long-term stability. Retain the remaining 30% as liquid reserves for flexibility or potential new ventures. Criteria for launching additional products should hinge on consistent month-over-month growth of at least 20% and a recurring profit margin above 30%. For example, if your dropshipping store hits this milestone for four consecutive months, allocate a portion of profits to explore adjacent niches or develop complementary digital products.

Momentum building is measured by establishing core metrics that clarify when to expand. Set a monthly minimum passive revenue goal. When a stream regularly brings in $1,000 in net monthly passive income with at least a 40% ROI (which is found by dividing net profit by total invested capital), it shows that it is ready to grow. Add dashboards that track customer acquisition cost (CAC), churn rate (if applicable), and lifetime value (LTV). Doubling down becomes the logical next step when CAC decreases while LTV and retention increase. For instance, if shifting 10% of the marketing budget from ads to affiliate partners boosts profits by 15%, that's a clear signal to reinvest more heavily in affiliate outreach.

Brand growth accelerates through targeted digital infrastructure upgrades. Start with a full website audit using tools like SEMrush or Ahrefs to eliminate slow-loading elements, fix broken links, and enhance on-page SEO. Integrate heatmap analytics — such as Hotjar — to identify high-engagement areas for optimized product placement or content upgrades. For newsletters, use MailerLite or ConvertKit to segment lists by customer interests, automate nurture sequences, and implement A/B tests for subject lines. Launch a biweekly value-driven newsletter packed with actionable tips, curated resources, and community spotlights. In community building, nurture engagement through private Facebook groups or Discord servers. Assign moderators, schedule weekly themed discussions, and incentivize contributor-generated content with monthly contests. These steps deepen audience loyalty and amplify organic reach.

Wealth measurement benefits from tangible autonomy metrics and scorecards. Define financial independence as covering core monthly living expenses (including housing, food, insurance, and personal savings) through passive streams. Use a "Freedom Scorecard" to track milestones: 25%, 50%, 75%, and 100% coverage. Create a table to map income streams to expense categories, helping spot areas for improvement. Balance financial goals with lifestyle by setting quarterly reviews to assess time spent on business maintenance versus leisure. Set a rule that major business decisions should not encroach beyond 20 hours of active engagement per month once mature systems are in place.

Robust Standard Operating Procedures (SOPs) enable the business to become systematized. Use tools like Notion or Google Docs to template every recurring task — listing product research steps, customer support responses, and content publishing schedules. Develop visual workflows for automations, such as connecting Shopify sales to Printful order fulfillment and Xero bookkeeping via Zapier. In digital product businesses, automate email delivery, license generation, and customer follow-ups. For content platforms, schedule posts with

Buffer or Hootsuite. Each process needs a clear trigger, action, and defined outcome for scalability.

Outsourcing demands a cost-benefit evaluation for every potential hire. Calculate the hourly cost of your time, then compare it to rates on platforms like Upwork for virtual assistants, copywriters, or technical specialists. If your time is valued at $80/hour and a VA charges $15/hour, delegating 10 hours/week immediately recaptures 65% of that value. Draft job descriptions listing required skills, daily tasks, preferred tools, and KPIs (key performance indicators). Use scorecards to assess new hires on criteria like responsiveness, accuracy, and initiative. For remote team management, adopt frameworks like daily Slack check-ins, weekly Asana project reviews, and monthly Zoom strategy sessions.

Exit strategies require understanding asset value. Digital businesses are commonly valued at 30–45x average monthly net profit. To sell a blog generating $2,000/month, a typical range is $60,000–$90,000. Explore licensing your brand, content, or digital products with clear royalty structures (e.g., 10% of gross sales) and defined term lengths. Decide on the optimum scale for an exit by monitoring peak profitability and market trends, ensuring you sell during heightened demand or automation maturity.

Continuous reinvestment and compounding returns lie at the heart of the wealth flywheel. Even modest annual growth rates — 10%–12% — turn $10,000 into over $31,000 in ten years. Chart your "time-to-freedom" based on expenses replaced by passive streams, noting each milestone when a new stream covers another core cost. This creates a living scoreboard motivating consistent effort and smart decisions on the path to sustainable, automated, and freeing wealth.

Now that we know how to effectively combine and manage different sources of passive income by mastering them, reinvesting wisely, and using efficient systems, we can confidently create a lasting way to achieve financial freedom. By thoughtfully selecting complementary income sources, applying disciplined time management, and leveraging automation and outsourcing, aspiring entrepreneurs can scale their wealth while maintaining balance and clarity. This chapter lays the foundation for expanding income with intention, reinforcing that true financial independence comes from steady growth, careful planning, and continuous optimization — empowering readers to take deliberate steps toward lasting prosperity beyond the constraints of traditional work.

HELP THE NEXT DREAMER BREAK FREE

Every insight we share can become a **stepping stone** for someone else searching for *freedom.*

Have you ever wished you had a *trusted guide* when trying to break free from the endless cycle of **trading time for money**?

Picture an aspiring entrepreneur, a burned-out professional, or a parent longing for *more time with their family* — someone who knows there must be a better way but feels overwhelmed by all the noise online. Your reflections on ***Passive Income Mastery*** could give them the clarity and courage to take their *first step.*

If this book helped you **understand passive income more clearly**, *sparked an idea* for your first income stream, or inspired you to think bigger about your financial future, I'd be honored if you would leave a short, honest review.

Your feedback not only supports my work — it also guides future readers who may be standing right where you once stood, *uncertain but hopeful.* Even a few sentences can **ripple outward**, helping others find the tools and confidence they need to reclaim their time and build *real freedom.*

Thank you for reading, reflecting, and sharing your journey. **Your words carry more power than you may realize.**

CONCLUSION

As you reach the end of this book, pause for a moment and reflect on the journey you have begun. The pursuit of passive income is not reserved for the fortunate few, nor is it a speculative gamble reserved for risk-takers. Rather, it is a disciplined, empowering process that anyone — with determination and commitment — can undertake. The blueprint is now in your hands, but its power lies in your willingness to act upon it. Passive income is not about chasing a fantasy of instant riches or abandoning all structure overnight; instead, it is about building enduring assets, step by step, until your money works harder than you do. It is the transformation from striving to thriving, from simply earning to consciously creating a life that serves your purpose and ambitions.

At the core of this approach is a profound shift in mindset. Many adults have been conditioned to see themselves exclusively as consumers or employees, bound to trade hours for dollars and to wait for others to set the limits of their financial destiny. This book has challenged you to reframe that narrative. You are invited to become a creator — to invest time and ideas into ventures that generate value long after your initial effort. You are encouraged to evolve into an investor — someone who sees opportunities where others see uncertainty and who builds systems and assets rather than watching passively from the sidelines. Most importantly, you are learning to transition from earning for survival to building a future where you can reclaim your time, direct your energy, and choose how you live every day.

Let us briefly revisit the path you have traveled throughout these chapters. In the early pages, you laid a critical foundation by identifying your "why" — the deeper motivation behind your desire for passive income — and clarifying your specific financial goals. This goal-setting process was more than a box to check; it was an act of taking ownership over your life's trajectory. With this clarity, you began constructing the scaffolding on which all subsequent actions would rest.

You've now explored a wide range of income streams, uncovering real-world strategies, analyzing risks and rewards, and reviewing practical steps for implementation. Whether you were drawn to the steady returns of dividend-paying stocks, the creative potential of digital products, the transformative opportunities in crypto assets, or the timeless wealth-building power of real estate, one truth became clear: there's no single formula for freedom. Each asset class comes with its own advantages and demands. You gained insights into earning royalties from intellectual property and content revenue, examined how to automate and scale online businesses, and explored emerging trends that are redefining how people earn beyond hourly wages. Across all these paths, one theme remained constant: lasting wealth and autonomy depend on building assets that continue to pay you — even while your focus shifts elsewhere.

The final section equipped you with advanced concepts necessary for sustained growth — how to stack multiple streams, scale them intelligently, and automate processes to minimize ongoing effort. Here, true freedom comes into view, not just as a financial state, but as a holistic transformation of daily living. Diverse, resilient portfolios protect your income from market shifts and personal setbacks alike, while automation and outsourcing free up space for creativity, relationships, and meaningful pursuits.

As you close this book, remember that there are infinite ways to build passive income, each uniquely suited to your strengths, interests, and circumstances. There is no universal right answer — only the path that aligns with your skills, resources, and vision for your ideal lifestyle. Whether you thrive on writing, coding, investing, teaching, or building communities, the modern economy offers countless entry points for generating lasting, automated wealth. Your job now is not to seek perfection or certainty but to select a single starting point and give it concrete shape.

Action must follow intention. Perhaps you have long dreamed of publishing your knowledge in an ebook, launching a video channel, acquiring your first rental property, or purchasing a basket of dividend stocks. Now is the time to commit to that first step. Create your outline. Record your introduction. Open an investment account. Begin researching your target market. Progress, not perfection, will propel you forward. Every imperfect first step sets the stage for incremental growth. Momentum emerges not from inaction, but from small wins repeated consistently over time. Let repetition become your ally as you refine your processes and expand your portfolio. Obstacles and setbacks are natural; resilience is developed through action and reflection, not hesitation.

Do not underestimate what is at stake in your decision to pursue passive income. At its heart, this blueprint is not merely a financial strategy — it is a means to reclaim agency over your most precious asset: time. Imagine mornings that begin gently, without alarm clocks dictating your routine. Envision the flexibility to travel widely, pursue creative passions, or spend time with loved ones, unencumbered by the requirement to ask permission or schedule vacation days. Imagine yourself contributing to causes you care about, confident that self-sustaining assets are meeting your essential needs in the background. Passive income is about unlocking options, reducing stress, and amplifying your impact on your terms.

Throughout this process, keep sight of your original purpose — your freedom number, the tangible milestone that represents both security and possibility. That number may signify the chance to leave a draining job, support a family, or simply regain balance between work and life. Whatever your unique aspiration, let it guide your decisions and reinforce your commitment during challenging moments. Each step, however incremental, moves you closer to that vision of independence and fulfillment.

Finally, remember that the journey toward financial freedom does not have to be lonely. Countless others are charting similar paths, experimenting with new models, and overcoming obstacles by sharing experiences and insights. You are invited to connect with like-minded individuals, leverage resource hubs, and contribute your voice to communities dedicated to sustainable wealth-building. Stay engaged by joining our newsletter, accessing free tools, and participating in forums designed to keep you accountable and inspired. Nothing accelerates progress like mutual encouragement and shared learning. Share your journey openly, for your story may inspire someone else to begin their transformation.

The blueprint is in your possession. Every principle, tool, and strategy outlined in these pages is ready to serve you. Do not let fear or uncertainty delay your pursuit of freedom. Take a bold first step today. Keep learning, keep building, and keep stacking your income streams until you have not only achieved your goals but surpassed them.

You've got the blueprint. Now build the life no one can take from you.

PART TWO

INVESTING 101

A BEGINNER-FRIENDLY GUIDE TO INVESTING IN THE STOCK MARKET, INDEX FUNDS, REITS, RENTAL PROPERTIES, CRYPTO, AND MORE—BUILD A POWERFUL, DIVERSIFIED PORTFOLIO WITH MINIMAL RISK AND EFFORT

INTRODUCTION

Do you remember the first time someone told you about investing? Maybe you pictured crowded stock exchanges with people in suits or imagined you needed thousands of dollars just to get started. For a lot of us, investing can seem like something reserved for the ultra-wealthy, people with finance degrees, or those who read The Wall Street Journal over their morning coffee. But here's an important truth: investing isn't just for 'them.' It's for you — whether you're a college student learning how to stretch your paycheck, a freelancer eager to grow your side hustle savings, or someone who's simply curious about building a brighter financial future.

To start investing, you don't need a specific job title, a significant amount of spare cash, or years of research experience. You need the courage to learn and take the first step, even if it feels scary. No matter where you're starting from, this book is designed to guide you, at your speed, toward real financial empowerment. If you've ever felt overwhelmed by confusing jargon or found yourself believing that investing is risky, complicated, and out of reach, you're not alone. These are common myths that hold far too many people back from taking control of their money.

Let's address one of the biggest obstacles right away: the fear that you don't know enough to invest wisely. Maybe you've heard stories about friends who lost money in the stock market, or perhaps news headlines make investing sound unpredictable and scary. Here's what you might not realize: not investing comes with its own set of risks, ones that are far more certain over the long term.

Take a moment to think about what happens when you leave your money sitting in a regular savings account. It feels safe, right? The money is there whenever you need it, and you might even earn a little bit of interest. But while your balance sits quietly, something else is happening behind the scenes — something called inflation. Every year, prices for things like groceries, rent, and transportation tend to go up, sometimes by only a small amount, sometimes by much more. Over time, this means the money you worked hard to save actually buys less and less. That $1,000 you put away today might be worth just $900, or even less, in real purchasing power ten years from now.

What does this mean for your dreams — owning a home, traveling, retiring comfortably, or simply enjoying freedom from financial stress? It means that relying solely on traditional savings accounts or stashing cash under your mattress isn't enough to keep pace with your life goals. Growing your wealth isn't just about accumulating money; it's about protecting your future self from missed opportunities. And that's where investing comes in.

Investing is often misunderstood as a gamble or a luxury. In reality, it is one of the smartest, most practical tools available to anyone who wants to shape a secure and meaningful future. When you invest, you put your money to work so you don't have to work forever. Thanks to the power of compounding — the process by which your investments generate returns, and then those returns generate even more returns over time — even small, consistent steps add up to significant progress. You don't need to start with large sums of money or proprietary knowledge. Whether you can set aside $5 a week or a few hundred dollars a month, you have options. Investing involves taking a long-term perspective, making well-informed decisions, and allowing time to take its course.

So why haven't more people embraced investing early? One reason is that myths and misinformation are everywhere. Maybe you've been told that investing is only for people with extra income to spare. Maybe you believe that if you're not a math whiz or a financial planner, you're bound to make costly mistakes. Or maybe you simply feel like all the talk about stocks, bonds, and mutual funds sounds like a foreign language. These beliefs are understandable, but they're also outdated. The truth is, most successful investors started out just as uncertain as you might feel right now.

Throughout this book, we'll break down these barriers together. You will learn why investing is not just possible but essential, regardless of your current financial situation or background. We'll translate unfamiliar terms into plain English and focus on practical steps that fit your lifestyle. Whether you have a steady job, juggle multiple gigs, are paying off student loans, or are saving for a big goal, there's a place for you in the world of investing. You do not need to have a lot of money to begin. You do not need to understand every corner of the market before taking action. What you do need is a willingness to move beyond old fears — and a commitment to your future.

Imagine feeling confident when opening your banking app, seeing your investments steadily growing, and knowing you're actively creating choices for yourself down the road. Think about being able to support causes you care about, take career risks, or retire earlier than you thought possible. None of this requires perfection. All it takes is a mindset shift and a little guidance, which you'll find in the pages ahead.

Here's what you can expect as you move through this book: First, you'll discover why investing matters — not just for Wall Street, but for everyday people trying to get ahead. We'll explore the real impact of inflation, show you why keeping money in low-interest accounts may be costing you more than you realize, and share stories of individuals who started with modest sums and saw life-changing results. Along the way, you'll find powerful evidence to replace old myths with new facts. By the end of our journey, you'll be equipped to recognize opportunities, weigh risks smartly, and make choices that align with your unique goals.

This book is your toolkit for changing the way you think about money and your ability to build wealth. Each chapter is crafted to meet you where you are, offering straightforward advice without overwhelming you. You'll find checklists, examples, and practical tips to help you take concrete steps — at your pace — toward a more secure future. You have the power to decide how quickly and how far you want to venture into the world of investing.

Ultimately, my goal is to help you feel prepared — not just to invest, but to take charge of your entire financial journey. No more feeling stuck or intimidated by complicated systems. Together, we'll simplify the process, clear away confusion, and put the power back in your hands. Investing is for everyone, and that includes you.

Welcome to a new chapter in your financial story. Let's begin.

THIRTEEN
THE BUILDING BLOCKS OF INVESTING

Have you ever wondered what it really means to invest, or why some people seem to grow their money steadily over time while others struggle to get ahead? Maybe you've heard the term "compound interest" tossed around but aren't quite sure how it works or why it matters. Or perhaps you feel uncertain about how much risk is too much when putting your money into stocks, bonds, or other opportunities. If these questions sound familiar, you're not alone.

Many adults starting out with investing face the same challenges — figuring out where to begin, understanding the balance between risk and reward, and learning how to make their money work for them without constant supervision. This chapter will help you build a solid foundation by explaining key concepts: what investing truly is, how compounding accelerates growth, why aligning risk with your comfort level matters, and what types of income different investments can generate. With clear examples and straightforward language, you'll gain the confidence to approach investing thoughtfully and take greater control of your financial future.

UNDERSTANDING INVESTING AND THE POWER OF COMPOUND INTEREST

Investing is putting your money to work so it can grow. Instead of allowing your cash to remain idle in your bank account while earning minimal interest, consider using it in ways that could generate higher returns. At its heart, investing is about making your money help you build wealth rather than only relying on your paycheck.

Picture someone who likes a particular company, maybe one that makes eco-friendly products. They believe this company will sell more in the future and make greater profits. By buying shares, or pieces of the company, this person becomes a partial owner. If the company does well, its value can increase, and so does the value of the shares. If the company also pays a portion of its profits to shareholders through dividends, that's an extra reward on top of any price increase.

Consider someone else who buys a house with the idea of renting it out. The rent each month provides regular income, while over the years the house could rise in value. If the owner sells it for more than they bought it for, that's an additional profit.

Think about bonds, which are like loans you give to governments or companies. In exchange for lending your money, they agree to pay you interest regularly and return your original investment later. Many people like bonds because of their steady stream of income.

There are also those who might invest by starting a small business — a coffee shop on a busy street, for example. The money spent on the shop is an investment. If the coffee shop thrives, profits can be much larger than the original amount put in.

What sets investing apart from saving is the way your money behaves. Saving is like storing your cash in a box — it stays safe but doesn't do much. When you invest, your money is actively working for you in the world. For example, if you put aside $1,000 in a savings account that pays 0.5% interest per year, you'll have $1,005 at the end of the year. But if you invest that same $1,000 in a business or shares in a growing company, you have a chance of making much more, even though there's some risk involved.

Take the case of a rideshare driver who wants to build a safety net. If they put away a portion of each week's earnings in a high-interest account or buy a small number of shares every month, their money isn't just set aside — it's potentially positioned to grow. Gig workers, freelancers, and young professionals often need their money to stretch further, and investing helps by offering the potential for higher returns than simple saving.

The driving force behind wealth growth in investing is the extra income it can generate. When you buy a rental property, those monthly payments from tenants start adding up, and over time, so does the property's value. When you hold shares in a company, you might receive dividends and watch your investment grow in value. What really accelerates wealth is reinvesting those returns — using the extra income from investments to make even more investments. It's like planting seeds that keep giving fruit and using some of that fruit to plant even more seeds.

There's a big difference between investing for quick wins versus thinking long term. Some individuals aim to achieve success by strategically timing the market or following rapidly evolving trends. But real wealth tends to grow over years, not days. This long-term perspective enables compound interest to function effectively.

Compound interest is when your earnings themselves start earning money. Imagine you invest $1,000 in a fund that grows at 7% each year. After one year, you'd have $1,070. Instead of taking out the extra $70, you leave it invested, so the next year it's 7% of $1,070, giving you $1,144.90. Year after year, your investment grows faster because you're earning returns not just on the money you put in, but also on all the profits that have built up. See how those numbers stack up over time:

Year	Value at 7% Growth
1	$1,070
5	$1,403
10	$1,967
20	$3,870

Starting early is important because compound growth gets stronger with time. Small amounts can grow into substantial sums if left invested and allowed to build on themselves.

There are many reasons people invest. Some want security for the future, like saving for retirement. Others hope to buy a home or pay for a child's education. Common places to put investment money include shares of companies, bonds, real estate, and starting or investing in businesses. Each works in a slightly different way, but all share the goal of turning today's money into more tomorrow.

Investing is simple: choose where to put your money, watch how it performs, and decide when to use your gains. Time is one of your most powerful tools. The longer you let investments grow, the more chance they have of multiplying. But every opportunity comes with its set of risks, and weighing them is always part of the investing journey.

BALANCING RISK AND REWARD: FINDING YOUR COMFORT ZONE

Investing often feels like putting your money on a see-saw. On one side, you find safety and certainty, but likely with small returns. On the other, you have chances for higher returns, but with the risk that things might not go as planned. This balance is called risk versus reward, and every investor must decide where they feel comfortable sitting.

In the world of investing, risk means the likelihood that you could lose money or that your investment won't do as well as you hoped. For example, placing your money in a savings account is very safe. The big banks rarely fail, so you can be sure your money will be there tomorrow. But the trade-off is that your money grows very slowly — barely more than a few pennies for each dollar over a year. This is low risk, low reward.

Consider another option: stocks. When you buy a stock, you become a part-owner in a company. If the company does well, so does your investment. It can grow quickly, sometimes doubling or tripling in a few years. But the company could also face problems and its value may drop, which means you could lose part of your investment. This is higher risk, higher potential reward.

Risk comes in many forms. It's not just about losing money because a company goes out of business. Some of the most common risks include:

Risk Categories in Investments

Risk Type	What It Means	Example
Market Risk	The chance your investment goes down because the market drops	Stock prices fall during an economic slump
Inflation Risk	The danger that rising prices will eat into your investment's value	Low-yield bonds may not keep up with inflation
Liquidity Risk	The risk that you can't quickly convert your investment into cash	Selling real estate can take months

Each type of investment carries its own mix of these risks. For example, government bonds are less affected by market ups and downs, and you can usually sell them quickly, so they carry less risk overall. But they don't pay much and may not keep up with inflation. Cryptocurrencies, on the other hand, change value quickly, are harder to predict, and might be tough to sell in a panic. The potential for big gains is there, but so is the chance of big losses.

Deciding how much risk to take should start with a look at your own financial situation and feelings about loss. This is called risk tolerance

— how much you're willing to stomach the ups and downs. Some people happily ride out wild swings in the hope of bigger gains. Others want to sleep well at night knowing their money is safe, even if it grows slowly.

Assessing Your Risk Tolerance

A few questions can help you decide where you stand:

- How would you feel if your investment lost 20% of its value in a year?
- Are you counting on this money soon, or can you leave it untouched for five years or more?
- Do you have stable income and savings to fall back on?
- What are your problems and goals — growing wealth, saving for a house, or planning for retirement?

Risk tolerance depends on personal factors. Younger investors sometimes accept more risk because they have time to recover from losses. Someone older, or planning to buy a home soon, may need to be more careful. Stable jobs and steady income let you handle more ups and downs. If you depend on your investments for daily living, playing it safe is generally better.

Matching Investments to Your Comfort Zone

Picture two friends, Amy and Ben. Amy is 25, starting her first job, and wants long-term growth to buy a home in ten years. She can handle more risk, so her portfolio holds mostly stocks and some bonds. Ben, 50, earns a good salary but wants to retire soon. He's more cautious, putting his savings mainly in government bonds and some savings accounts.

Diversifying across different types of investments can also spread risk. Instead of betting everything on one company or property, spreading money into stocks, bonds, savings, and maybe a small slice of something riskier like real estate or mutual funds helps cushion losses if one part falls behind. This mix helps manage risk while still offering room for growth over time.

Passive income strategies reward patience with steady returns. Investments in dividend-paying stocks or rental properties may offer fewer wild swings but provide ongoing cash flow. High-yield savings accounts create slow, reliable growth. Each method fits a unique risk/reward preference, emphasizing that there's no single right answer. The important part is knowing your comfort zone, assessing your priorities, and choosing matching investments you can stick with.

PASSIVE VS. ACTIVE INCOME: BUILDING WEALTH THROUGH INVESTING

Many people dream of waking up to money earned while they slept. This is the promise behind passive income, which stands in contrast to active income — each playing a different role in the journey toward financial independence. Understanding how they differ, and how investing helps transition from one to the other, is crucial for crafting a sustainable wealth-building plan.

Active income refers to money you receive in exchange for your effort, time, or skills. Consider a freelance web designer who gets paid per project or a young professional working a full-time job for a monthly salary. If they stop working, their income halts. This exchange of hours for dollars means your earning potential is bound tightly to the hours you can physically or mentally contribute. Side hustles, like pet-sitting or driving for a rideshare service, also fall under active income. They may fit flexibly into your schedule, but they still require presence and energy.

Passive income operates differently. It's income generated with minimal day-to-day involvement. For example, when a web designer invests in a small apartment and rents it out, the monthly rent payments become passive income. Another scenario involves purchasing shares in a company — receiving dividend payments without doing the daily work of running the business. These income streams typically require upfront work, capital, or creativity but continue generating money with little ongoing attention.

Passive income streams are pivotal for long-term financial growth because they help to decouple your earning capacity from your time. As life circumstances change, having income that isn't directly tied to hours worked increases flexibility. In retirement, or during a career break, passive earnings can maintain your standard of living. For side-hustlers or freelancers facing inconsistent workloads, passive income provides a financial cushion and peace of mind when active projects slow down.

Establishing passive income sources usually requires a significant initial effort. Purchasing a rental property demands research, legal paperwork, and sometimes renovation. Creating a digital course or self-published eBook involves a heavy burst of upfront creativity and technical work before it can generate ongoing sales. Even investing in dividend stocks or real estate investment trusts (REITs) means researching, choosing, and managing investments and reviewing performance periodically. Passive income is rarely effortless at the outset — success often comes down to the quality of the initial setup and the diligence invested in risk assessment.

A few traditional passive income opportunities available through investing include:

- Rental real estate: Buying property and earning income through monthly rent payments
- Dividend-paying stocks: Earning a share of company profits regularly, just for holding stock
- Peer-to-peer lending: Funding loans for other individuals or businesses in exchange for regular interest payments
- REITs: Investing in real estate portfolios that pay out a portion of proceeds as dividends

These avenues illustrate that investing acts as an entry point for making your money work for you. The degree of direct involvement still varies. Owning a single-family home and acting as a landlord can be more management-intensive than investing in a mutual fund, where your role is mostly to monitor and rebalance your portfolio.

The relationship between effort, time investment, and income potential is central to both income types. Active income may deliver faster returns when starting out — a freelance writing gig pays within weeks, while investment property might not yield positive cash flow for months. Passive income, on the other hand, can compound over time; a diversified portfolio steadily grows through reinvested dividends or appreciation in property value. However, the time it takes to build meaningful passive income streams is often underestimated, as is the persistence and learning curve involved.

Evaluating passive income opportunities involves looking closely at risk, potential returns, and personal resources — skills, capital, and available time. A side-hustler with marketing expertise might build a blog that earns ad revenue, while someone with savings might prefer dividend stocks or REITs. Key questions to ask include: What is the minimum investment? How stable is this source of income? What risks could disrupt it? How easily can it scale if I want to increase my returns?

Diversification becomes crucial, both as a safeguard and as a way to expand total passive income. Instead of relying on a single rental property, investing in different asset classes — like stocks, real estate, and digital products — mitigates the risk of one stream failing. For young professionals, balancing a few manageable passive sources alongside active work is a realistic path to stability.

Passive income is sometimes thought of as a myth or "easy money," yet most people discover it's built on consistent effort, wise investing, and a patient mindset. Recognizing the benefits and limitations of both active and passive income allows everyone — from freelancers to full-time employees — to better match their resources to income opportunities and to lay the groundwork for financial security and freedom.

Now that we have explored the core ideas of investing — from how your money can grow through compound interest to finding a balance between risk and reward and understanding the difference between active and passive income — you are better prepared to take the next step. With this foundation, you can begin making informed choices about where to put your money, tailored to your goals, comfort with risk, and lifestyle. Remember, investing is not about quick wins but steady growth over time, giving you the power to build financial security and create income streams that work for you. As you move forward, keep learning, stay patient, and use these principles to shape a plan that fits your unique journey toward financial independence.

FOURTEEN
LAYING YOUR FINANCIAL GROUNDWORK

Have you ever found yourself wondering where your money goes each month, despite earning a steady paycheck or juggling multiple gigs? Perhaps you feel like saving or investing is out of reach because bills and expenses appear to pile up faster than you can keep track. For many adults starting their financial journeys, the challenge isn't just making money — it's understanding how to manage it well enough to build something lasting.

Setting clear goals and knowing how much to save or invest feels overwhelming when the basics aren't in place. Without a solid handle on your budget, unexpected costs, or growing debt, investing can seem risky or confusing. This chapter will guide you through establishing a strong financial foundation by mastering budgeting, protecting yourself from emergencies, handling debts intelligently, and aligning your investment plans with your personal goals and timelines. Taking these steps first helps turn scattered income into intentional growth, creating confidence and control as you begin building your financial future.

MASTERING BUDGETING TO FIND INVESTMENT CAPITAL

Earning money is only the first step; knowing exactly how much reaches your bank account each month lays the foundation for smart budgeting. If you work a regular nine-to-five, your paycheck may be steady, but it's still worth adding up your total income — after taxes — before making any plans. Freelancers and gig workers should average their earnings from the past several months to establish a reliable baseline. Even if income varies, reviewing your lowest-earning month helps you create a "worst-case scenario" budget that protects you from overspending.

Once your monthly income is clear, the next step is tracking expenses. Start by gathering statements from your bank, credit cards, or budgeting apps. List every regular bill — rent, utilities, phone, subscriptions, insurance, groceries, and transportation. Then add variable expenses: dining out, entertainment, shopping, and other costs that fluctuate. Whether you prefer pen and paper, a spreadsheet, or a digital app like Mint or You Need a Budget (YNAB), consistency is what matters most. Many people find that a simple spreadsheet with columns for "Income," "Fixed Expenses," and "Variable Expenses" keeps everything organized and easy to review.

After tracking a full month of spending, patterns begin to emerge. Maybe your coffee runs total $45 a month, or you're still paying for a streaming service you rarely use. This is where budgeting shifts from passive record-keeping to an active tool. Beside each category, mark expenses as "Needs," "Wants," or "Could Cut." These distinctions make it clear which costs are essential and which ones offer opportunities to redirect money toward your goals. For example:

Category	Amount	Type	Change
Rent	$800	Need	–
Groceries	$200	Need	–
Streaming	$15	Want	Could Cut
Restaurants	$90	Want	Reduce
Gym	$25	Need	–
Ride Shares	$30	Want	Reduce

This clear format helps visualize where money can be redirected. Maybe by skipping two restaurant dinners and dropping a streaming site, you free up $40 each month.

To make budgeting work long-term, consider using the 50/30/20 rule. Under this system, 50% of your after-tax income covers "Needs," 30% goes to "Wants," and the remaining 20% is dedicated to "Savings/Investing." For someone earning $2,000 monthly, the breakdown would look like this:

- Needs: $1,000
- Wants: $600
- Savings/Investing: $400

Plugging these percentages into your spreadsheet or app keeps spending in check and ensures investing happens every month. Digital tools with "goal" features, like PocketGuard or YNAB, even let you assign your investing amount as a recurring monthly target, giving you a clear number to hit.

Life isn't always predictable, and budgets need flexibility. If some months bring extra freelance work or overtime, decide in advance how much of that windfall will bolster investments. On the other hand, if your work is seasonal and some months are lean, setting aside buffer funds in better months can even things out. For irregular expenses like car maintenance or holiday gifts, estimate the annual cost, divide by twelve, and save that amount each month, smoothing out the bumps.

As your budget takes shape, the power of small changes emerges. Let's say you find $30 a month to invest — maybe that's a couple fewer movie tickets or resisting one impulse buy. Over a year, that adds up to $360. If invested regularly, those small sums grow — not just from your contributions, but from investment growth over time. It's easy to overlook these "extra" dollars when they're sitting in checking accounts, but tracking turns them into opportunities.

Imagine Sarah, a young professional with a $2,600 monthly take-home pay. Before budgeting, her savings account rarely grew. After tracking her spending, she realized $120 a month vanished on rideshares and food delivery. Cutting back to public transit and cooking three extra dinners weekly freed up $85 a month. She set up an automatic transfer — $50 to a basic investment account and $35 toward emergency savings. By the end of the year, she'd invested $600 and saved $420, all without feeling deprived.

Budgeting uncovers not just investment potential but also any gaps in emergency funds or warning signs of growing debt. Seeing a negative balance or frequent overdrafts is a prompt to cut more deeply or seek extra income before committing to investments. Proper budgets build confidence — making saving, spending, and investing intentional, not accidental. Each dollar you redirect strengthens your financial safety net and lays the groundwork for future growth.

BUILDING YOUR FINANCIAL SHIELD: EMERGENCY FUNDS AND DEBT MANAGEMENT

Unexpected expenses often arise when least expected, making it vital to build protection before investing. A solid financial shield is created through two key elements: maintaining an emergency fund and managing debt wisely. These act as buffers, protecting you from life's uncertainties while laying the groundwork for future investment success.

Understanding Emergency Funds

An emergency fund is money set aside specifically for genuine financial emergencies — situations you cannot predict or avoid. True emergencies include job loss, unexpected medical bills, urgent home or car repairs, or family crises that require immediate attention and resources. Non-emergencies are expenses you can plan for, like vacations, new gadgets, or sale events. Recognizing this difference helps avoid depleting your savings for nonessential reasons.

To determine the right size for your emergency fund, calculate your essential monthly expenses: rent or mortgage, utilities, groceries, transportation, insurance, and minimum debt payments. Multiply this total by three to six months as your target range. For example, if your monthly expenses total $2,500, then an emergency fund should fall between $7,500 and $15,000. A single person with stable employment may lean towards three months, while someone with dependents or variable income may choose the higher end.

Building your emergency fund rarely happens overnight. Instead, treat it as a goal to achieve in small, regular steps. Start by budgeting a set portion of your income each month, even if it's just $50 or $100. Set up an automatic transfer to a dedicated savings account, so the money moves before you spend it elsewhere. Celebrate milestones to stay motivated, such as reaching your first $500 or $1,000.

Accessibility is the main priority for emergency savings, not high returns. The money needs to be readily available when needed, so keep your fund in a high-yield savings account or a money market account. Avoid investing your emergency fund in stocks or other assets where its value could fluctuate or where withdrawals might take days to process.

Debt Management: Types and Strategies

Debt comes in many forms, but not all debt is created equal. High-interest debt — such as credit card balances, payday loans, and some personal loans — can quickly grow out of control if left unchecked.

Manageable debt includes low-interest student loans, mortgages, and some car loans, especially when payments fit comfortably in your budget and interest rates are moderate.

Prioritizing which debts to pay down first is crucial. Focus on high-interest debts before low-interest ones. Credit cards, often charging between 16% and 25% interest, cost you much more over time than the 3% to 5% you might pay on a mortgage. If you owe $5,000 on a credit card at 20% interest, you'll pay $1,000 a year just in interest. Compare this to potential investment returns: if your investments are projected to earn 7%, but your debt costs you 20%, you're actually losing money by investing rather than paying off this debt.

Some believe you can start investing immediately, even with high-interest debt, but this often erodes the benefits of your investments. It's typically wiser to eliminate these expensive debts first, then move to investing once you're spending less on interest and have reduced financial stress.

Several proven strategies help reduce debt effectively:

- **Avalanche Method:** Pay minimums on all debts, then put any extra money toward the debt with the highest interest rate.
- **Snowball Method:** Pay minimums on all debts, then target the smallest balance first to gain momentum from early wins.
- **Debt Consolidation:** Combine your debts into one loan with a lower overall interest rate for easier management.

A table helps illustrate these strategies:

Method	Focuses On	Pros	Cons
Avalanche	Highest interest	Saves most on interest	May take longer to see progress
Snowball	Smallest balance	Quick wins boost motivation	May pay more in interest
Consolidation	All debts into one	Streamlines payments, possible savings	Qualification required

How Emergency Funds and Debt Work Together

Imagine you start investing without an emergency fund. Suddenly, an unexpected car repair arises, costing $1,200. With no cash reserve, you swipe your credit card, adding to a balance with 22% interest. This new debt means future investment contributions have to cover both interest losses and possible lost investment growth.

With an emergency fund, the repair is paid promptly, and investments remain untouched and growing. Emergency funds also reduce stress and keep you from selling investments at a loss during a crisis.

A balanced approach often works best while building your foundation. For instance, if you have $300 a month to spare, you might put $200 toward credit card debt and $100 toward growing your emergency savings. This steady effort builds protection and steadily reduces liability, ensuring you're ready to invest confidently when the time comes.

Common myths suggest any savings are enough or that investing should always come first. In truth, a proper emergency fund and smart debt management provide the foundation for safe, sustainable investing. They enable you to navigate financial challenges, prevent additional debt, and enter the world of investing with assurance and stability.

DEFINING FINANCIAL GOALS AND ALIGNING THEM WITH TIME HORIZONS

When setting financial goals, the timeline for when you'll need the money is just as important as the amount. In investing, this timeline is called your "time horizon." Different time horizons shape your investment choices and the amount of risk you should consider. Time horizons generally fall into three categories: short-term, medium-term, and long-term.

Short-term goals mean you expect to use the money within three years. Common examples include saving for a vacation, building an emergency fund, or putting money aside for a car. Protecting this money from unexpected losses is crucial because we will need it soon. Even small downturns in the market can hurt if you need your funds quickly. That's why those with short-term goals usually focus on low-risk investments like savings accounts, certificates of deposit (CDs), or high-yield money market funds. These vehicles tend to offer modest returns but very little risk.

Medium-term goals are those with a three- to ten-year time frame. Examples are saving for a house down payment in five years, planning for a wedding, or building a college fund for a child who is starting elementary school. This period is long enough to consider more growth-focused investments but not so long that you can fully ignore risk. Investors often balance stable options with higher-return possibilities, such as a mix of bonds and conservative stock funds. This approach allows some room for ups and downs, with time to bounce back from moderate setbacks but not from severe losses.

Long-term goals look ten years or more into the future. Retirement is the classic example, but so are funding a newborn's college education or creating lasting wealth for your family. Over these extended timelines, you can weather the short-term fluctuations of the stock market. History shows that while stocks might occasionally drop sharply, they have trended upward over longer spans. For instance, according to the S&P 500's performance between 1926 and 2023, the average annual return was about 10%. While that doesn't mean every year was positive, it illustrates the long-term growth potential. Because of this, long-term investors are generally able to take on more risk by investing a larger portion of their money in stocks and stock-based funds.

There is no universal risk tolerance. Some individuals experience sleeplessness due to minor losses, whereas others don't mind fluctuations if they anticipate a larger future reward. However, your investment time horizon can help guide what amount of risk is appropriate. If you need your money soon, it's usually best to avoid riskier investments. If your goal is years away, you may have more capacity to handle short-term losses in exchange for greater possible gains.

Linking your goals to the right time horizon gives your plan structure. It can help to use a simple table or list like this:

Goal	When Needed	Time Horizon	Ideal Options
Buy a car	1 year	Short-term	Savings account, CD, money market
Down payment on house	5 years	Medium-term	Bond funds, balanced portfolios
College for newborn	18 years	Long-term	Stock funds, index funds
Open a business	2 years	Short-term	Cash, short-duration bonds
Retirement	30 years	Long-term	Stock funds, retirement accounts

To get started, make a list of your specific goals and estimate when you'll need the money for each. Assign each goal to one of the time horizon categories. Consider your own feelings about risk and use that understanding to choose investments that feel comfortable.

Another key concept is compound interest. Money you invest earns returns, and over time, those returns can generate even more returns, creating a snowball effect. For instance, if you invest $10,000 in a stock fund with an average annual return of 8%, after 3 years (short-term) you'll have about $12,600. Over 10 years (medium-term), the amount grows to nearly $21,600, and in 30 years (long-term), it can balloon to over $100,000. This shows why letting your money grow longer can make such a dramatic difference.

Different life events require different horizons and strategies. If you're saving for a house in just a few years, it makes sense to keep the money safe and stable. If you're building a college fund for a newborn, time is on your side — a stock fund or a 529 plan might give your investments room to grow. For a teenager's college fund, you'll lean toward safer, more stable options because there's less time to recover from downturns.

As your goals and timelines shift, update your investment strategies. For instance, as retirement nears, move some funds from stocks to more stable vehicles like bonds or cash, reducing risk as your need for the money grows closer. Periodically review your goals to confirm your investments still fit your needs and update your plans as your life changes.

Now that you have learned how to create a clear budget, build an emergency fund, manage debt wisely, and align your investment choices with your goals and time frames, you are equipped to lay a strong foundation for your financial future. These steps help transform money management from a source of stress into a tool for growth and security. By mastering these basics, you can confidently begin investing with a plan tailored to your needs, protecting yourself from unexpected setbacks while steadily working toward the life you want. As you move forward, remember that small, consistent actions add up over time — setting you on a path to financial success and peace of mind.

FIFTEEN
MEET THE ASSETS — WHAT YOU CAN INVEST IN

Have you ever wondered what exactly you're investing in when you put your money into stocks, bonds, or real estate? Many people hear these terms and feel unsure about how they actually work or why they matter. It can be confusing to know where to start or how to build a portfolio that balances growth and safety. What does it mean to own a piece of a company, lend money to the government, or invest in digital currencies? Why do some options offer steady income while others promise bigger rewards but come with more risk?

Understanding the different types of assets available is key to making smart investment choices. This chapter will introduce you to the main categories of investments and explain how each one functions, their roles, and how they fit together to help you reach your financial goals. Whether you're saving for retirement, a home, or simply want to grow your wealth steadily, knowing what you can invest in sets the foundation for success.

TRADITIONAL INVESTMENT VEHICLES: STOCKS, BONDS, MUTUAL FUNDS, INDEX FUNDS, AND ETFS

Buying a share of stock is like owning a small piece of a company. If you buy one share of Apple, you truly own part of it. Stocks represent ownership, and companies sell these shares to raise money. When people talk about "the stock market," they're talking about all the shares from thousands of companies traded each day. Investors can choose stocks from renowned brands like Nike, Microsoft, or Starbucks.

Stocks make money in two ways: if the company pays a part of its profits to shareholders, called dividends, or if the stock's price rises and you sell it for more than you paid. For example, if you buy a share of a retailer like Walmart for $100 and sell it later for $120, you make a $20 profit. Dividends are usually paid out every three months. Some companies don't pay dividends and instead reinvest profits to grow the business, which can also make the stock price increase.

Owning stocks means taking more risk. If a company does poorly, the value of your stock can drop. Markets can swing, and occasionally a company's stock price falls even when it's doing everything right. The stock market as a whole can move up or down quickly, so stocks are best for people who can leave their money invested for at least five to ten years and handle ups and downs.

You don't need a fortune to buy stocks. Many online brokers let people start with as little as $10 or $25. Some even sell "fractional shares," which means you can buy part of a share if the price is high. Stocks are bought and sold on stock exchanges such as the New York Stock Exchange (NYSE) or Nasdaq, usually through an online account.

Stocks are popular with people who want their money to grow over time. Historically, U.S. stocks have returned about 7% per year after inflation, but this isn't guaranteed every year. Some years see strong gains; others see losses.

Buying a bond is like lending your money to a company or government. When you own a bond, you are the bank. In return, the borrower promises to pay you back later — the date is called "maturity" — and sends you interest payments along the way. Bonds are safer than stocks for most investors, but no investment is completely safe.

Governments, cities, and businesses all sell bonds. The U.S. government issues **Treasury bonds**, which are considered very safe. Companies sell **corporate bonds** to fund projects, and cities offer **municipal bonds** to finance things like schools or infrastructure. Each type carries a different level of risk, but all share one feature: they pay regular interest, usually every six months.

Bonds generate returns in two ways: through interest payments and by selling the bond for more than you paid. Most investors hold bonds for the steady income. Yields vary over time: U.S. Treasury bonds might pay 2–4% annually, while riskier bonds often pay higher rates. The main risks are that the borrower might default or that rising interest rates could reduce your bond's resale value before it matures.

Bonds typically require higher minimum investments, sometimes $1,000 or more. You can buy them through brokers or directly from the issuer, such as on the U.S. Treasury's website. Bonds are a solid choice if you want greater stability and a predictable income stream.

A **mutual fund** is like a shopping cart full of investments. Instead of choosing a single stock or bond, you buy a share of a mutual fund, and a professional manager selects dozens or even hundreds of investments for you. The fund gathers money from many investors, pools it, and buys assets according to its stated goals.

There are mutual funds that focus on growth (seeking stocks that may rise quickly), income (choosing bonds or dividend-paying stocks), and balanced funds (mixing stocks and bonds for a smoother ride). For example, a growth fund might own shares of Google, Netflix, and Amazon, while an income fund might buy government and corporate bonds.

Mutual funds make money from the same sources as stocks and bonds: rising prices, dividends, and interest. Some require $500, $1,000, or even less as a minimum investment, making them accessible for beginners. They're bought directly from mutual fund companies or through online brokers.

A common myth is that mutual funds are just for experts. In fact, they're a simple way for everyday people to spread out risk and let someone else handle day-to-day decisions. Beginners often like mutual funds because they can get a diversified mix with one purchase.

Stocks have more growth potential but more risk. Bonds are steadier but don't grow as fast. Due to their diversification, mutual funds help lower the risk associated with single investments. By mixing stocks, bonds, and mutual funds, an investor gets both growth and some safety, which is the foundation of a strong investment plan.

These three tools each play an important role, and together, they help people work toward goals like buying a home, sending kids to college, or building retirement savings. Holding stocks for several years can yield significant rewards, while bonds provide stability, and mutual funds simplify investing for all investors. As mutual funds package investments together, they lead naturally to even more efficient options across markets, setting the stage for exploring index funds and exchange-traded funds, which make broad diversification and low costs possible for all investors.

REAL ESTATE & REITS: PROPERTY INVESTMENTS FOR EVERY INVESTOR

Real estate investing means putting your money into property to earn a return, either through rental income, property value growth, or both. There are different ways to get involved with real estate, from buying a house or an apartment directly to investing in pooled funds such as Real Estate Investment Trusts (REITs). Each approach has its own benefits, risks, and requirements.

Investing directly by owning property is the most traditional way to invest in real estate. You can buy residential homes, like single-family houses, or commercial buildings, like office spaces and stores. In residential rentals, you can often get started with a 20% down payment on a mortgage. For example, if you buy a $200,000 home, a down payment might be $40,000 plus closing costs. Once you own the property, you can rent it out and collect monthly payments. Suppose your mortgage, taxes, and maintenance cost $1,100 per month, but you rent the home for $1,400 per month. That gives you $300 per month in passive income, before occasional repair costs or vacancies. Over time, the property may also rise in value — a concept known as appreciation. If your $200,000 house grows to $250,000 over ten years, that's a $50,000 gain when you sell, not counting transaction costs.

Direct ownership has clear risks. Tenants can miss payments or damage the property. The house could sit empty between renters, adding stress or lost income. You'll be responsible for repairs, paying property taxes, and dealing with issues like leaky roofs or broken appliances. These property management tasks require involvement or the hiring of a property manager, which comes with additional fees. Selling a house takes time, so real estate is not as straightforward to cash out of as stocks or bonds.

REITs provide a way to invest in real estate without owning a building yourself. REITs are companies that buy, manage, or finance real estate and trade on stock markets like regular shares. You might invest as little as $1,000 in a publicly traded REIT through a brokerage account. Your money joins that of thousands of other investors, and the REIT uses it to buy things like shopping malls, hospitals, or apartment complexes. You receive dividends, typically paid every quarter, from the rental income and profits generated by these properties. For instance, if you invest $1,000 in a REIT yielding 5%, you'd expect about $50 per year in payouts, though this is not guaranteed and depends on real estate market health.

REITs are popular because of their liquidity. You can buy and sell shares easily, unlike selling a property. However, because they trade on public stock markets, REIT prices can fluctuate quickly, exposing you to market swings. REIT income is often taxed as ordinary income, not at the lower long-term capital gains rate, so tax planning is important.

Some investors look into real estate crowdfunding platforms. These websites let multiple investors pool small amounts — often $500–$1,000 — into a single project. You might help finance a new apartment complex or hotel, sharing in rental income or project profits. Crowdfunding lets you invest smaller amounts and diversify across several projects. But it often comes with less liquidity than REITs, as your money could be locked up for several years until the project finishes or sells. These deals generally require less day-to-day involvement but carry higher risks if the project fails.

Real estate mutual funds offer another way to diversify. These funds invest in a mix of REITs or real estate-related companies. With as little as $250, you can spread risk over a wide range of properties, and professionals will manage the investments. Liquidity is high, but like REITs, market swings can affect values.

The main benefits of real estate are steady income, possible price growth, and low correlation with stocks and bonds, which can protect your portfolio during stock market downturns. Many investors appreciate getting monthly cash flow from rentals or quarterly dividends from REITs. But real estate is usually more complex than stocks or bonds and has unique risks, such as property damage or real estate market cycles that affect values. Economic downturns can mean falling property prices and lower rent collections.

Practical risk management helps. For direct ownership, keeping a cash reserve covers repairs and vacancies. For REITs or funds, diversification across different property types lessens risk. Understanding local real estate trends and not overpaying for a property are key to long-term success.

This blend of income, appreciation, and diversification makes real estate a useful part of an investment portfolio. With options from hands-on property to easy-access REITs, even small investors can take advantage of opportunities in the real estate market.

CRYPTOCURRENCY: DIGITAL INVESTING FOR BEGINNERS

Digital money is something most people already use every day, whether it's paying with a bank card or sending funds through an app. Cryptocurrency works like digital money too, but it is different because it doesn't rely on banks or governments. Instead, it uses secure technology called blockchain, which is like a digital ledger or notebook everyone can see, but no one can change without others seeing it too. Each cryptocurrency, like Bitcoin or Ethereum, runs on its version of this ledger.

Cryptocurrency, often just called "crypto," is a type of digital asset. It is created and stored electronically. The most well-known example is Bitcoin, started in 2009. Bitcoin's idea was to allow people to send money over the internet, directly from one person to another, without a bank in between. Others soon followed, such as Ethereum, which does something similar to Bitcoin but also lets people make agreements, or "smart contracts," right in the code.

How Cryptocurrency Works: The Basics

Think of each Bitcoin as a special token that lives on its online ledger. If you "own" a Bitcoin, the ledger records that your digital wallet controls it. When you send Bitcoin to someone, imagine moving a digital token from your wallet to theirs. This transaction is recorded with many others, forming a secure and permanent log. Millions of computers worldwide keep copies of this log, known as the blockchain, making it very hard for anyone to cheat or change history.

Ethereum works in a similar way, but it's not just about sending tokens. People can write rules called smart contracts — little programs that live on the Ethereum blockchain. These rules can automatically move Ethereum tokens between users once certain conditions are met, much like a digital vending machine that only releases a soda after you put in the right amount of money.

Why People Invest in Cryptocurrency

A few factors make cryptocurrency attractive to investors:

- **Potential for Big Returns:** Bitcoin, for example, was once almost worthless and later reached values in the tens of thousands of dollars per coin. This potential has drawn many investors hoping for high profits.
- **Limited Supply:** Bitcoin has a built-in rule: only about 21 million will ever exist. Some other cryptocurrencies have similar limits, which can make them seem scarce and possibly more valuable.
- **New Technology:** Other applications of the blockchain technology, which powers cryptocurrencies, include tracking supply chains, recording property ownership, and storing medical records. Some investors see this as a sign that these systems have staying power.

Common Concerns and Myths

Many newcomers worry that cryptocurrency is only for tech experts or criminals. In reality, anyone can buy and use cryptocurrency with a little guidance. Another myth is that it is completely anonymous — every transaction is actually recorded on the public blockchain, though identities are hidden behind wallet addresses.

Some people also think cryptocurrencies are "get rich quick" schemes. While some have made a lot of money, prices often swing wildly, and there are no guarantees of profit. Unlike stocks or real estate, cryptocurrencies don't have underlying companies or physical assets, which makes prices hard to predict.

Getting Started: Buying, Storing, and Trading Safely

1. **Choose a Reputable Exchange:** Websites like Coinbase, Kraken, or Binance let you buy and sell Bitcoin, Ethereum, and other digital coins. These exchanges require you to create an account, verify your identity, and link a bank account.

2. **Store Your Crypto Securely:** You can leave your coins on the exchange (online wallet), but for higher safety, move them to your own "wallet." There are two main wallet types:

Method	Description	Security Level
Hot Wallet	Online app or website	Moderate
Cold Wallet	Hardware device, disconnected from web	High

Cold wallets, like USB sticks, protect your coins from online hacks.

3. **Protect Your Information:** Use strong passwords. Turn on two-factor authentication (2FA), which requires a code sent to your phone or an app before logging in. Never share your private keys (the secret codes that control your coins).

Building Cryptocurrency into a Portfolio

Cryptocurrencies are riskier than traditional investments. Most experts suggest new investors keep crypto to a small slice of their overall portfolio. A common recommendation is 1-5% of your investments. This way, if prices drop sharply, your losses won't overwhelm your finances, but if values rise, you still benefit.

It's important to research before buying any coin. Look for facts: what problems does the cryptocurrency try to solve, who is running the project, and how many coins will exist? Reliable information can be found on official project websites and trusted investment sites.

Risks and Rewards

Crypto values can change dramatically in a short time. Values might be driven by news, government decisions, or changes to the technology itself. For example, a government ban or a major hack can cause prices to crash. On the other hand, adoption by big companies or positive technical updates can send values soaring.

In the long term, some investors see cryptocurrency as a way to balance other types of investments, like stocks or bonds. With careful research, safe habits, and realistic expectations, cryptocurrency can play a role in a modern investment plan, as long as you manage your risks wisely.

Now that you understand the key investment options — stocks, bonds, mutual funds, real estate, and cryptocurrency — you're better equipped to start building a balanced portfolio that fits your goals and comfort with risk. Each asset class offers unique benefits and challenges, and combining them thoughtfully can help protect your money while aiming for growth over time. Whether you choose to invest directly or through funds, begin small, stay informed, and remember that investing is a journey best approached with patience and clear purpose. With this foundation, you're ready to explore strategies that make your money work harder for you and move confidently toward your financial future.

SIXTEEN
THE POWER OF DIVERSIFICATION

Have you ever felt uneasy about putting all your money into a single investment, only to watch its value drop unexpectedly? Maybe you've heard stories of friends who rushed to buy the latest hot stock and ended up losing most of what they put in. It's natural to wonder if there's a safer way to invest — one that doesn't depend on guessing which asset will perform best or avoiding sudden losses.

Investing can feel overwhelming, especially when markets shift without warning and the future seems uncertain. People new to investing often worry about risk and how to protect their hard-earned money while still aiming for growth. Understanding how to spread your investments thoughtfully can ease some of this anxiety and help build confidence. This chapter explores why diversifying your investments is an essential strategy to manage risk and work toward steady returns. We'll look at how spreading money across different types of assets can create balance, reduce surprises, and support your financial goals over time.

UNDERSTANDING DIVERSIFICATION AND ASSET ALLOCATION

Imagine holding a basket full of eggs while walking down a bumpy path. If you stumble and all your eggs are in that one basket, every single egg might break. But if you split them between several sturdy baskets, a single slip may only cost you a few. This simple idea perfectly illustrates diversification in investing. Diversification means spreading your money across different types of investments instead of putting it all in one place. The goal is to reduce the risk of losing everything if one investment performs poorly.

Many beginners think investing is about picking one winning stock or following the latest hot tip. While these approaches can sometimes work, they also carry significant risk. Diversification offers a proven way to manage that risk by reducing the impact of any single investment that underperforms. Consider an investor who puts all their savings into one technology company. If that company struggles, their financial future is in danger. By contrast, someone who invests in a mix of technology, healthcare, real estate, and bonds is less likely to lose everything, even if one sector has a difficult year.

History provides many examples of the power of diversification. During the tech bubble of the early 2000s, investors who held only technology stocks saw their savings vanish. Those who also owned other investments, such as bonds or non-tech stocks, avoided the worst losses. Diversification acts like a shock absorber. When one part of the market declines, others may hold steady or even rise, softening the impact.

The benefits of diversification go beyond just avoiding big losses. Diversification addresses one major area of risk. By investing in different things that don't always move together in price, you lower the chance that all your investments will lose value at the same time. This creates the potential for more steady, reliable returns over time. Imagine a portfolio with stocks, bonds, and some real estate. If the stock market plunges, bond prices might rise as investors seek safety, and real estate values might remain stable or change slowly. The different pieces work together to balance out gains and losses.

Market ups and downs are a natural part of investing. Diversification helps cushion against market volatility, the sudden changes in prices that can be unsettling for investors. Imagine a new investor during a market downturn. If their portfolio includes many types of assets, they're less likely to panic when one part drops in value. Industry-specific events, like a scandal at a large oil company or new technology disrupting an old business model, are as well less threatening when your investments are spread across various sectors. This approach doesn't remove all risk, but it helps reduce surprises.

There are a few myths about diversification that can make beginners hesitate. Some people think only the rich can afford to diversify, but today, anyone can do it. Many apps and investment products let you invest small amounts across different assets. Others believe diversification is too complex, requiring profound knowledge or expert help. While investing can be complicated, the basics of diversification are straightforward and easy to put into practice. Some assume you have to know a lot about global markets. In reality, even beginners can diversify by investing in index funds or exchange-traded funds (ETFs), which already contain a variety of companies, industries, or even countries.

Diversification looks different depending on what you invest in. Spreading your money between stocks, which represent ownership in companies, and bonds, which are loans to companies or governments, is a beneficial starting point. You can also include real estate through real estate investment trusts (REITs), which allow you to invest in property without buying buildings yourself. Adding international investments broadens your reach and helps protect against problems in any single country. Diversifying by industry and by the size of companies — mixing large, stable firms with smaller, growing ones — offers more layers of protection.

Thinking about risk is important for investors. There are two main kinds: systematic risk and unsystematic risk. Systematic risk affects the whole market, like a global recession or a sudden rise in interest rates — no amount of diversification can avoid it completely. Unsystematic risk, however, is tied to specific companies or industries.

Diversification is a powerful tool for lowering unsystematic risk. By diversifying your investments, setbacks in one area are less likely to harm you. The end result is risk-adjusted returns, meaning you're putting yourself in a position to earn rewards that make sense for your level of risk.

Diversification matters because it offers protection, steadier growth, and a more confident path toward your goals. You don't need to be wealthy or an expert. All it takes is the willingness to spread your investments broadly and let time — and the power of diversification — work in your favor.

SAMPLE PORTFOLIOS FOR EVERY INVESTOR

Many investors wonder how to turn the theory of diversification into a plan they can actually use. By looking at sample portfolios for different goals, it's possible to see how different asset mixes cater to varying levels of risk, time horizons, and life stages. Let's explore three portfolio types — the conservative, the balanced, and the growth-oriented — and see how each one works in the real world.

A conservative portfolio centers around stability and capital preservation. The main aim is to minimize losses, even if it means lower returns. Imagine an investor with $10,000 whose main goal is to preserve capital for a near-term need, like a home down payment or retirement in a few years. The allocation might look like:

Asset Class	Percentage	Dollar Amount
Government Bonds	50%	$5,000
High-Grade Corporate Bonds	20%	$2,000
Dividend-Paying Stocks	15%	$1,500
Broad Market Index Fund (ETF)	10%	$1,000
Cash or Money Market	5%	$500

Most of the portfolio lies in government and high-quality corporate bonds. These tend to offer safety in tough times and generate predictable income. Dividend-paying stocks provide modest growth and regular cash flow, acting as a cushion when the market stumbles. A broad market ETF captures a slice of the equity market, but at a small enough portion that it won't cause big waves when stocks swing. Keeping a cash buffer lets the investor cover unexpected needs without selling investments at a difficult time. Someone choosing this model usually has a low risk tolerance, a shorter time frame, or may be managing funds for a big purchase within three to five years. They value peace of mind over chasing after higher returns. This portfolio may not grow as quickly as others in volatile markets, but it rarely falls behind — even when stocks decline sharply, bonds and cash cushion the impact.

A balanced portfolio aims for moderate growth but adds a reasonable degree of safety. This approach blends stocks and bonds to balance out risk and return. Suppose a person plans to invest $10,000 for 10 years, such as saving for a child's college education or a future house. Their allocation might be:

Asset Class	Percentage	Dollar Amount
U.S. Stocks (ETF or mutual fund)	35%	$3,500
International Stocks	15%	$1,500
Bonds (mix of U.S. Treasuries and corporates)	40%	$4,000
Real Estate Investment Trust (REIT ETF)	5%	$500
Cash/Short-Term Instruments	5%	$500

About half the portfolio stays in bonds and cash, limiting downside during downturns. Adding both U.S. and international stocks enables participation in market growth from different regions, spreading risk. REITs bring extra diversification because real estate often moves differently from stocks or bonds. This arrangement typically serves investors who are midway in their careers or have longer-term ambitions, like building wealth for retirement over a decade or more. While this portfolio can decline in a rough market, its blend of assets helps it recover and smooths out wild swings. The result is an evenhanded approach — higher potential than a conservative model, but enough defense to avoid sleepless nights during market turbulence.

Seeking the largest possible gains means building a growth-oriented portfolio. With bigger risk comes the potential for bigger reward — and a sturdier stomach for market ups and downs. Suppose a younger investor in their 20s or 30s is putting $10,000 to work for retirement that's decades away. Their mix might look like:

Asset Class	Percentage	Dollar Amount
U.S. Stocks (ETF or mutual fund)	45%	$4,500
International Stocks	25%	$2,500
Small Cap & Emerging Market Stocks	15%	$1,500
Sector ETFs (e.g., tech, healthcare)	10%	$1,000
Bonds/Cash	5%	$500

Here, stocks dominate. The focus is on high-growth options — U.S. and international, plus a slice in small-company and emerging-market stocks for more adventurous upside. Adding sector funds increases the chance for above-average returns if certain industries surge. Bonds and cash form a tiny buffer for emergencies. Because the goal is decades away, short-term losses are less worrying, and there's time to recover from downturns. This model supports long-term wealth building and is ideal for someone with plenty of time, a higher risk tolerance, and no immediate need for the money. In good years, the growth portfolio can race ahead, but it will also swing wider than the others during downturns.

Each of these portfolios demonstrates practical diversification. By blending asset types, regions, and even market segments, they spread out risk and position for suitable returns. These models are not strict rules — they offer templates that can be tweaked based on personal priorities, financial goals, and stage of life. The right mix helps investors face uncertainty with confidence and the optimism that comes from a smart, diversified plan.

MASTERING REBALANCING TECHNIQUES

A well-constructed portfolio needs regular maintenance to stay on track and achieve its goals. Even if all the right choices are made in the beginning — spreading investments between stocks, bonds, and other assets — real-world changes will shift how much each asset makes up in the portfolio. Over time, those shifts can turn a balanced portfolio into one with more risk than intended or with too little growth potential. The simple act of rebalancing means checking and correcting the mix so it matches the plan. Certain signals let investors know when it's time to rebalance.

Time-based triggers are among the most common. Many investors set a schedule to rebalance their portfolios at regular intervals, such as quarterly or annually. The idea is that regardless of what the market does, a check-in happens at set times. This method makes portfolio management part of a routine, so busy periods or market excitement do not cause it to be forgotten. Still, a lot can happen between those calendar dates, so some people use percentage-based triggers instead. This approach sets a rule like "If any asset class moves more than 5% away from its target allocation, it's time to act." For example, if a portfolio is designed to be 60% stocks and 40% bonds, and rising stock prices raise stocks to 68%, that's an 8% drift — enough to trigger a rebalance. Life events also sometimes call for a change. Getting married, receiving an inheritance, or planning for retirement can all mean a portfolio should be rebalanced based on new goals, financial situations, or risk tolerance.

Breaking down the rebalancing process makes it less daunting. The first step is to assess the current allocation. This involves listing each asset and its current value, then calculating the percentage that each one represents in the overall portfolio. For instance, in a $10,000 portfolio where $6,800 is in stocks and $3,200 is in bonds, stocks now make up 68% of the portfolio rather than the intended 60%. The second step is to identify which assets need adjustment. The aim is to bring the allocation back in line with the targets, so it's clear whether to trim some investments or add to others. Finally, make strategic buying and selling decisions. If stocks have grown beyond their target, some are sold and the proceeds are used to buy other assets that have fallen behind, like bonds.

A real-life example makes this clearer. Consider a portfolio designed with 60% stocks ($6,000) and 40% bonds ($4,000). After a year, the stock market has performed well, and stocks are now worth $7,200, while bonds have grown to $4,200. The new total is $11,400. To see whether rebalancing is needed, calculate the new percentages:

Asset	Current Value	Portfolio %	Target %
Stocks	$7,200	63.2%	60%
Bonds	$4,200	36.8%	40%

Stocks have drifted up by 3.2%, while bonds are now underweight. To restore the target balance, calculate 60% of $11,400 = $6,840 for stocks and 40% of $11,400 = $4,560 for bonds. This means the investor should sell $360 from stocks ($7,200 - $6,840) and use that money to buy bonds, bringing the portfolio back to its original ratio.

Many investors notice challenges when rebalancing. Taxes can come into play if selling certain assets triggers capital gains, which may result in a tax bill. Transaction costs — small fees for buying or selling investments — can add up, especially in smaller accounts, so it's wise to check if the costs outweigh the benefits. Emotional barriers often arise, too, since it feels counterintuitive to sell assets that are performing well and buy those that are lagging. However, rebalancing is necessary because otherwise, market swings could throw the portfolio off course. Worry about market timing can also creep in, since no one wants to buy high or sell low. Sticking to a set schedule or clear rules helps remove guesswork and emotion from the process.

Staying organized makes rebalancing easier. Many brokerages and investment platforms offer tools that show a current asset allocation at a glance and automatically highlight when balances stray from targets.

Some apps and spreadsheet templates let users track their progress, sending reminders or generating easy-to-understand charts. A simple worksheet where investors log each asset, its value, and its percentage of the portfolio can be helpful, especially for those who want a hands-on approach. These resources save time and mean there's less risk of missing important signals.

Regular rebalancing keeps portfolios healthy, on purpose, and less swayed by emotion or sudden market moves. Consistent habits and the right tools help investors stick to their plans and manage risk while aiming for long-term growth.

Now that you understand how diversification spreads risk and how rebalancing keeps your investments aligned with your goals, you're better equipped to build a portfolio that grows steadily and weathers market ups and downs. By mixing different asset types and regularly reviewing your allocation, you can protect yourself from sudden losses while aiming for returns that match your comfort with risk. This approach is not just for experts or the wealthy — anyone can start small and grow smarter over time. With these tools in hand, you're ready to take confident, thoughtful steps toward a secure financial future.

SEVENTEEN
GETTING STARTED – YOUR FIRST INVESTMENTS

Have you ever felt overwhelmed by the many choices and steps involved in starting to invest your money? Maybe you've glanced at investment apps or heard stories about people growing their wealth through the stock market, but the details often seem confusing or intimidating. Questions like "Which platform should I trust?" or "How much money do I need to get started?" might be holding you back from taking that first step.

Starting with investing can feel daunting because there are so many options and considerations. From picking the right brokerage to understanding account types and managing deposits, it's easy to feel unsure about where to begin. This chapter will guide you through these early decisions and actions, helping you gain clarity and confidence as you open your first investment account, make your initial investments, and set up a plan that keeps your money working for you over time.

SELECTING YOUR BROKERAGE OR INVESTMENT PLATFORM

Many first-time investors feel unsure where to begin, faced with a maze of platforms and brokerages promising everything from low fees to cutting-edge technology. Understanding the differences between traditional brokerages, online investment platforms, and mobile-first apps will help you make a confident start.

Traditional brokerages often have long-established reputations, offering personal advisors and physical branches. These can be valuable for those who appreciate one-on-one support and are willing to pay for more comprehensive service. The rise of online platforms and mobile-first apps, however, has made investing far more accessible. Online platforms typically provide web-based dashboards, educational tools, and digital support systems at lower costs. Mobile-first apps, designed primarily for smartphones, feature simple interfaces and instant notifications that appeal to younger, tech-savvy investors who value speed and convenience.

When choosing where to begin, focus on the features that matter most to beginners. Start with the user interface: a clean, intuitive layout helps prevent mistakes when placing trades or checking your portfolio. Platforms like Robinhood and Wealthsimple stand out for their straightforward design and ease of navigation. Educational resources are equally important. Look for beginner guides, glossaries, tutorials, and in-app quizzes that builds your understanding step by step. Fidelity and Vanguard, for instance, are known for their comprehensive learning centers and interactive tools. Finally, strong customer support can make all the difference when you need help. Check whether live chat, phone assistance, or community forums are available, and how quickly you can expect a response.

Fee structures are an important part of the decision. The move toward commission-free trading — where buying and selling stocks or ETFs no longer incurs a per-trade charge — has changed the landscape, making investing more affordable than ever. Robinhood, E*TRADE, and SoFi Invest have adopted this fee model. However, pay special attention to account minimums and maintenance fees. Some platforms require a set amount to open an account (for example, Vanguard traditionally required $1,000 for some mutual funds), while others allow you to begin with just a few dollars. Ongoing maintenance or inactivity fees can eat into profits, especially for those who aren't planning frequent trades.

Security is non-negotiable. Look for two-factor authentication, SIPC or FDIC insurance in the United States, or similar protections elsewhere, and transparent data encryption policies. Reputable platforms will display their regulatory compliance and explain how your assets are protected. Global investors can access research platforms from their respective countries. Interactive Brokers and Saxo Bank, for instance, are popular internationally and support multiple currencies and languages, making them ideal for those outside the U.S. or for users interested in international markets.

The types of investment products a platform offers can shape your long-term strategy. Some platforms specialize in stocks and exchange-traded funds (ETFs), appealing to those who want instant access to fast-moving markets. Mutual funds, available on Fidelity, Charles Schwab, and Vanguard, work well for those seeking diversified, managed portfolios. Newer apps like Acorns or Stash offer automatic investing through "round-ups" or curated portfolios, catering to users who want a passive, set-and-forget approach.

Practical Tools for Choosing an Investment Platform

A structured comparison can clarify your options. Use the table below to evaluate platforms side-by-side:

Feature	Platform A	Platform B	Platform C
User Interface	Clear/Simple	Complex	Modern
Educational Resources	Extensive	Limited	Moderate
Fees/Commissions	Low/Free	High	Free
Account Minimums	None	$500	None
Investment Products	ETFs/Stocks	Mutual Funds	All types
Global Access	Yes	No	Yes
Security	Strong	Standard	Strong

Ask yourself:

- Am I comfortable navigating the app or website without confusion?
- Does the platform offer the educational help and customer service I need?
- What fees and minimums apply, and do they fit my budget?
- What kind of investments do I want to start with?
- Is this platform usable and legal in my country?

Watch out for red flags such as unlisted fees, poor customer reviews, weak security statements, or platforms lacking regulatory oversight. Examples like Robinhood appeal to those wanting no commissions and a mobile interface, while Schwab attracts with a broad product list, educational breadth, and robust customer care. Acorns is suitable for anyone looking to invest spare change with minimal effort.

Choosing the right platform comes down to aligning features with your strategy, support needs, and investment products. Some investors need constant support and robust educational resources, while others value low fees and global accessibility. As you narrow your choices, prepare to gather the necessary documents and meet any account requirements to open your first investment account smoothly in the next stage.

OPENING AN ACCOUNT AND MAKING YOUR FIRST INVESTMENT

Choosing the right investment platform marks the beginning of your journey, but opening and funding your account is where plans start to become reality. Opening an account typically starts with an online form. Most platforms ask for your name, contact details, Social Security number, and employment information. This may feel personal, but it's a legal requirement to protect your account and comply with regulations. Expect to provide a clear copy or photo of a government-issued ID, like a driver's license or passport, to verify your identity. If you're setting up an IRA or other specialized account, you may also be asked for additional documentation, such as a beneficiary designation or evidence of current employment status.

Several account types are usually available for investing. The standard option is an individual brokerage account. This account works well for most beginners and is suitable if you simply want to buy and sell investments on your timeline. Some platforms offer joint accounts for couples or partners. Retirement accounts, like Traditional or Roth IRAs, come with tax advantages but also have stricter rules about deposits and withdrawals. Custodial accounts let parents invest on behalf of their children, while trust accounts serve more specialized needs. Each option is clearly labeled during the sign-up process, but it helps to know what fits your goals before moving forward.

Platforms often require an initial deposit to activate your account. Some well-known brokers, like Fidelity or Charles Schwab, let you start with no minimum — technically, you could open and leave the account unfunded for a while. Others, such as Vanguard, may require a $1,000 minimum for certain accounts. For beginners, starting with an initial deposit of $100–$500 is both manageable and meaningful, providing enough funds to explore basic investments without feeling overwhelmed.

Once your account is open, funding methods vary. Bank transfers (ACH), wire transfers, and checks are common, while some platforms now support PayPal or even debit cards. The default option is often bank transfer, where you securely link your checking or savings account to the investment platform. Linking your bank is straightforward: you enter your bank's routing and account numbers or log into your online banking through a secure connection provided by the platform. Many applications use encrypted integrations with major banks, so your login details are never stored. Bank transfers tend to be free and usually take one to three business days to process. Wire transfers might move money within the same day but often cost $15–$25 per transaction.

Typical Processing Times and What to Expect

After confirming your funding method, you'll usually see a pending deposit in your investment account within 24–72 hours. Most platforms clearly display the status of your transfer — look for messages like "deposit in progress" or "awaiting funds." Funds are often available for investing after the transaction settles, though some platforms offer instant deposit features for small amounts (e.g., up to $1,000 immediately) if you're using a linked bank account. Larger transfers, wires, or paper checks may require full clearing, extending the wait by a couple of business days.

Navigating Security Measures and Verification Steps

Security is a common concern for first-time investors. Most platforms require two-step verification — after entering your password, you'll be sent a code by email or text to confirm your identity. Some may ask security questions or use facial recognition if you're applying via mobile app. Account verification helps prevent fraud and unauthorized access. It's also normal to be asked for a selfie holding your ID or to answer a few quick questions from your credit history.

If paperwork is missing or a document image is blurry, expect a quick request for a re-upload, with clear instructions on what's needed.

Managing Obstacles and Making Funding Easier

Occasional snags are common. Banks may reject a link if your name doesn't match exactly, or a deposit may be held up if your account information is mistyped. Double-check details, use name formatting that matches your bank records, and keep funding amounts within daily limits to avoid holds. If your platform offers a test deposit — typically two tiny amounts under $1 — that's to confirm the account is yours. Enter those exact amounts when prompted to activate your link.

Recurring deposits are a helpful feature for building good habits. Most platforms let you set automatic transfers from your bank for a set amount on a weekly or monthly schedule. Starting with $25 or $50 per month makes investing routine and less intimidating, ensuring steady growth over time.

Once your deposit clears, your account will show available cash. You're now ready to purchase investments — from stocks to index funds. Some platforms offer instant investing with settled funds, while others may display a "settlement period" for new deposits. Watch for confirmation emails with details, and keep records of your transfer receipts for quick reference. Starting small makes the process less stressful, keeps risk low, and helps you build confidence before making larger investments.

AUTOMATING YOUR INVESTMENTS FOR LONG-TERM GROWTH

Automatic investing is a system where money leaves your bank account and moves into your investment account according to a schedule you set. Automatic investing puts your wealth-building plan on autopilot, eliminating the need to decide every month how much to invest — or worse, to forget to invest entirely. Your money works for you in the background, quietly growing without the need for daily attention or energy.

Setting up automatic investing has several valuable benefits, especially for people who feel busy, anxious, or overwhelmed by the idea of investing. First, automation removes emotion from the process. On tough days when spending might feel tempting, the money is already on its way to your investments. This approach prevents emotional decisions and keeps your strategy on track. Second, automatic investing helps build financial discipline. Regular contributions, no matter how small, turn into a steady habit that pays off over time. Third, it saves time and mental bandwidth, because there's no need to remember, calculate, or manually transfer money each time you want to invest. Finally, setting up a recurring investment plan takes advantage of the principle of dollar-cost averaging: by investing consistently, you spread your money over different market conditions instead of trying to time the market.

Most investment platforms and brokerage firms have built-in tools to help you automate your investments. Once you decide how much you want to invest and how often, you provide your bank account details and set the schedule. For example, popular apps like Fidelity, Vanguard, Robinhood, or Acorns let you choose an amount — say, $50, $100, or $200 — and pick how frequently you want that amount invested. The platform then moves your chosen money on your preferred schedule, either buying shares directly or adding to your account's balance for investment.

Common Automatic Investment Schedules

Frequency	Minimum Example	Typical User
Weekly	$25	Freelancers/gig workers, people with weekly paychecks
Bi-weekly	$50	Salary earners paid every other week
Monthly	$100	Most common for people with steady monthly income

If you get paid every Friday, you might set aside $25 to invest at the end of each week. This means you're investing $100 each month, which can add up to more than $1,200 a year. Someone with a biweekly paycheck could invest $50 every two weeks, matching deposits with pay periods to make managing cash flow easier. Monthly schedules are good for planning investments around rent and bills, which are due at the same time each month.

It's normal to have concerns about giving up manual control. People often ask, "What if my income sometimes drops?" or "What happens if I can't afford the scheduled investment one month?" The best automatic systems are flexible. Most platforms allow you to pause, lower, or adjust your deposit anytime. You can start small with as little as $10 or $25. Over time, as you see your balance grow and your confidence increases, you'll find it easier to bump up the amount.

To figure out what an appropriate automated amount looks like, start by listing out your repeating monthly expenses. Subtract your rent, utilities, groceries, and other necessities from your typical monthly income. The leftover is your pool for savings and investing. Choose a percentage or dollar amount that feels comfortable — sometimes that means starting with $25 or $50 a month. If you have an irregular or gig-based income, consider setting your automation to a lower base threshold, such as $10 weekly, then topping off manually at the end of a strong month.

Here's how this plays out in real life: Mia earns about $2,800 a month after taxes, with variable freelance jobs. She lists $2,100 worth of bills and essentials. That leaves $700 for savings, but with unpredictable months, she picks a safe amount of $25 per week, which works out to $100 per month automatically invested. In months with more gigs, she manually adds extra hours to her schedule.

Visualizing the Power of Compounding

Let's compare three automatic schedules for a $50 monthly investment at a 6% annual return over 10 years:

Frequency	Annual Total Invested	Est. 10-Year Value*
Monthly	$600	~$8,200
Bi-weekly	$1,300	~$17,600
Weekly	$2,600	~$35,200

*Assumes all contributions are invested regularly; market returns vary.

Adjusting automated investments is simple. As your income grows, update your plan every six months or after a raise. If you start at $25 per week, but next year you have a higher salary, consider increasing to $35 or $50. Even small increases accelerate long-term gains. If you ever need to pause, most platforms make it easy with just a few clicks.

Automation turns investing into a steady force for building wealth, even when life gets hectic. By picking a manageable schedule, adjusting as your situation changes, and taking advantage of technology, anyone can create a foundation for financial security that runs on autopilot.

Now that you understand how to select the right investment platform, open and fund your account, and set up automatic investing, you're well-positioned to take confident steps toward building your financial future. By choosing tools that fit your needs and automating your contributions, you simplify the process and remove many common barriers that hold beginners back. As you move forward, remember that investing is a journey — starting small, staying consistent, and adjusting your plan as life changes will help you develop habits that grow your wealth steadily over time. With these foundational steps in place, you are ready to explore more advanced strategies and watch your investments work for you, even when life gets busy.

EIGHTEEN
AVOIDING COSTLY MISTAKES

Imagine sitting at your kitchen table, watching the value of your investments drop day after day. You feel a knot in your stomach as headlines scream about market crashes and economic uncertainty. Suddenly, an urge takes over — you want to sell everything before you lose more. But in the rush to act, doubts creep in: Did I just make a costly mistake? How do others seem to stay calm and come out ahead?

Many new investors face moments like this, caught between emotions and choices that can change their financial future. Fear, the pressure to follow rising trends, and the temptation to react impulsively are common obstacles that can hinder even the best-intentioned individuals. Without knowing how to recognize these traps, it's easy to make decisions that erode hard-earned gains and slow progress toward building wealth.

This chapter covers the hidden challenges investors face and reveals why understanding these pitfalls is crucial. By learning how emotional responses and overlooked costs can quietly sabotage success, you'll gain clarity on how to navigate investing with confidence and caution. Recognizing these hurdles early empowers you to build habits that protect your money and set the stage for long-term growth.

OVERCOMING EMOTIONAL TRAPS AND THE MYTH OF MARKET TIMING

Many smart investment strategies unravel not because of lack of planning, but because of powerful emotions clouding judgment. The most common emotional traps investors fall into are fear, fear of missing out (FOMO), and panic. Each of these can prompt impulsive choices that derail even the most carefully crafted investment plans. By understanding these traps, recognizing their signs, and learning strategies to stay objective, investors can increase their chances of long-term financial success.

Fear: Market Downturns and Defensive Instincts

Fear is a survival instinct that alerts us to danger, but in investing, it often prompts people to flee the market when things get rough. When markets fall sharply, such as during a major correction or recession, negative headlines and steep portfolio losses trigger anxiety. Investors confronting a 15% drop in the stock market might immediately worry: Will I lose everything if I ride this out?

This fear usually leads to actions like selling stocks at a loss or moving money to cash as a protective measure. Real-world examples include the rapid sell-off during the early days of a financial crisis or news of a sudden global event. Investors often rush to exit, hoping to avoid further losses, but this often results in them missing the subsequent recovery. Research by behavioral economists like Daniel Kahneman has shown that people are wired to feel losses more deeply than gains, leading to risk-averse behavior during downturns.

The effects of giving into fear can be severe. By selling at the bottom, investors turn paper losses into real ones, missing out on future gains when the market rebounds. To counter this, investors should ask themselves: Am I acting because of short-term fear, or does the data warrant a long-term change? Taking a pause before reacting — such as committing to a 24-hour waiting period before any major investment move — can help bring anxiety levels down. Writing down the original reasons for your investments and checking if those fundamentals have truly changed offers clarity. A simple checklist can be helpful:

Self-Check	Response Needed?
Is this decision based on headlines?	Wait 24 hours
Are fundamentals still strong?	Stay the course
Am I following my long-term strategy?	Re-evaluate only if long-term goals shift

FOMO: Urgency and Herd Mentality

The fear of missing out, or FOMO, strikes hardest during hot investment booms. News of friends making quick profits in trending assets, or seeing a stock's value skyrocket overnight, creates this urgent need to join the crowd. Technology stocks in the late 1990s or cryptocurrencies in recent years are classic cases where investors felt compelled to buy in, afraid of being left behind.

FOMO often prompts investors to abandon their regular research or carefully planned strategies. Instead, choices are driven by hype, headlines, and social proof. This can lead to buying at inflated prices, just as excitement is peaking. Inevitably, the excitement cools and prices correct, leaving latecomers with potential losses.

To manage FOMO, it helps to pause and ask: Would I still invest in this asset if it wasn't popular? Does it align with my goals and risk tolerance? Writing down your reasons for investing can clarify if the decision fits your plan or is being shaped by envy or social pressure. Many successful investors recommend having a "cooling off" period for any investments inspired by trends. If after 48 hours the rationale still makes sense and passes your criteria, it may be worth considering. Otherwise, sticking to your personal investing guidelines keeps FOMO in check.

Panic: Sudden Changes and Hasty Choices

Panic is a more intense variant of fear, often seen during dramatic market swings over a very short period. When markets crash on breaking news or unexpected events — such as a country defaulting on its debt or a pandemic emerging — logic tends to fly out the window. The urge to act quickly can overwhelm any prior planning.

Investors in panic mode might rapidly sell off assets, shift everything into cash, or abandon their strategy entirely. Panic-driven trades are usually the result of feeling completely out of control. During the 2008 financial crisis, studies on investor behavior revealed that many who liquidated their investments during the height of fear missed the substantial recovery that followed, often waiting many years to regain their former wealth.

Building emotional resilience means preparing for volatility before it happens. Creating a written investment plan, complete with rules for when and how to rebalance, sets up automatic responses that override panic. Using reminder notes like "Don't make decisions at market extremes" or setting thresholds (e.g., only reviewing portfolios quarterly, not daily) also helps. Checking in with questions such as "Am I acting out of fear or informed analysis?" puts a pause on rash decisions.

Recognizing these emotional traps and having practical steps to manage them connects directly to long-term investing success. Emotional discipline supports the steady, consistent approach that research shows delivers better returns over time. Investors who learn to spot their triggers, establish personal guardrails, and stick to their plans can ride out market ups and downs much more effectively.

IDENTIFYING HIGH FEES, HIDDEN COSTS, AND OVERTRADING

Every dollar invested should work as hard as possible for its owner, but fees and hidden expenses can quietly siphon growth from a well-designed portfolio. Even low-sounding percentages, when stretched over years and applied to large sums, can snowball into significant reductions in wealth. Understanding these costs and minimizing their effect is at the heart of smart, cost-conscious investing.

Management Fees and Expense Ratios

Investment products, whether mutual funds or exchange-traded funds (ETFs), routinely charge management fees. These fees are typically stated as a percentage of assets under management, known as the expense ratio. For example, a fund with a 1% expense ratio charges $10 annually for every $1,000 invested. Larger portfolios mean higher absolute costs: $100,000 invested at 1% incurs $1,000 per year in fees, regardless of whether the investments perform well.

While 1% may not sound like much, compare it to a low-cost index fund charging only 0.10%. Over 30 years, the difference becomes dramatic. If both funds return an average of 7% before fees, $10,000 grows to about $54,300 with the 0.10% fund but only around $45,300 with the 1% fund — a difference of $9,000 just from fees. This gap widens further with larger amounts and longer horizons. The higher the fees, the more your compounding returns are reduced.

Fees don't end with expense ratios. Some investment products have sales loads — one-time commissions that can take 3% to 6% off the top when you buy, or when you sell. For a $10,000 investment, that's $300 to $600 gone before your money even has a chance to grow. Ask if the fund charges any entry or exit fees, and favor no-load funds whenever possible.

Hidden and Overlooked Costs

Not every cost shows up on a product sheet. Brokerage commissions, though lower today thanks to zero-commission trading on many platforms, can still add up for frequent traders or those using specialized products. Account maintenance fees — such as annual charges or inactivity fees — may quietly drain accounts, especially smaller ones or those held in specialized accounts like retirement plans.

Taxes loom large as a hidden cost. When investments generate interest, dividends, or realized capital gains, a portion may go to the government. For example, selling a stock that has doubled in value triggers capital gains tax, reducing your net profit. Frequent fund turnover inside actively managed funds can result in higher taxes passed along to investors, even if they haven't personally sold any assets.

Imagine a portfolio producing a pre-tax return of 7%. If annual taxes and hidden fees reduce this by just 1%, the long-term growth drops significantly. Compounded over 20 or 30 years, seemingly minor costs erode a substantial part of the total investment.

Ask for a breakdown of all potential account fees before investing. Review fund documents for trading costs and turnover rates. Use online fee calculators to estimate the total cost year by year. Always check if an account charges for paper statements, wire transfers, or other services.

The True Cost of Overtrading

Frequent buying and selling, often in pursuit of quick gains or to follow the latest trend, comes with a tangible cost. Each trade may incur commissions or spread costs (the difference between buying and selling prices). More importantly, short-term trades often result in short-term taxable gains, which are taxed at a higher rate than long-term holdings.

Research consistently shows that investors who trade often tend to underperform buy-and-hold investors. This underperformance comes from a combination of transaction costs, taxes, and the tendency for frequent traders to mistime the market.

Consider two investors, each starting with $50,000. One trades actively, making 20 trades a year at $10 per trade, plus incurring 1% in taxable short-term gains. The other makes only one or two trades annually and holds investments for the long term, paying little in commissions and enjoying the lower long-term capital gains tax rate. Over a decade, the active trader can lose thousands in extra costs and taxes while also risking lower market returns due to mistimed decisions.

A guiding principle is to trade only when there's a clear, rational reason — such as adjusting for major life changes, rebalancing, or responding to significant shifts in goals or risk tolerance. Before executing a trade, ask yourself: Does this move serve a long-term plan, or is it a reaction to short-term noise?

Cost-Conscious Investing in Practice

To build a cost-efficient portfolio, start by listing all possible fees for each investment option. Compare expense ratios, account fees, and likely tax implications. Use online tools like fee comparison calculators or portfolio analysis apps to see how small differences in cost add up over time. Ask advisors: What is the total cost of owning this investment for five, ten, or thirty years? Are there lower-cost alternatives with similar performance?

Focus on minimizing new trades. Set guidelines such as requiring a written reason for every trade or waiting a week before acting on any new investment idea. Favor diversified, low-cost funds or ETFs, and consider tax-efficient investment accounts. Regularly review statements for new or increasing fees.

Every percentage point saved grows your wealth faster. By making cost-awareness a habit, investors keep more of what they earn and avoid mistakes that quietly drain progress toward their goals.

SPOTTING SCAMS AND AVOIDING BAD ADVICE

Every investor hopes to grow their money safely, but the investment world contains hidden traps. While high fees can eat away at your returns, deliberate scams and bad advice can cause even bigger losses. Understanding the types of fraud and how to protect yourself is just as important as choosing the right stocks or funds.

Recognizing Investment Scams

Investment scams often use the excitement of high profits or new opportunities to draw people in. Some of the most common schemes include Ponzi schemes, pump-and-dump operations, and fake investment opportunities:

- **Ponzi schemes** promise big returns with little risk and generate "profits" by using money from new investors to pay earlier participants. Bernie Madoff's massive fraud is a well-known example, but many smaller versions target ordinary people every year.
- **Pump-and-dump operations** involve hyping up a stock (often through social media or emails) to drive up its price, then the fraudsters sell their shares, making a profit while everyone else is left with worthless stock.
- **Fake investment opportunities** come in many forms — phony real estate deals, fraudulent cryptocurrency schemes, or imaginary startup investments. Scammers create slick websites and convincing materials to make these fake investments seem real.

Spotting Red Flags

Even though scammers routinely update their tactics, there are recognizable warning signs that wise investors learn to spot. Some common red flags include:

- **Promises of guaranteed returns:** No honest investment can promise you a specific profit, especially high or risk-free returns. "No risk, high reward" should always set off alarms.
- **High-pressure sales tactics:** If someone insists you must act immediately or you'll miss out, they may be trying to prevent you from thinking things through or asking questions.

- **Unlicensed or unregistered advisers:** Many scams are operated by advisers or companies with no legal credentials or official registration.
- **Complex, difficult-to-understand strategies:** Scammers often try to confuse victims with jargon or complicated explanations so you feel embarrassed asking questions.
- **Exclusive or time-sensitive opportunities:** If only you are "special enough" for an opportunity, or there's a ticking clock, step back and verify the claims.

Evaluating Financial Advisers and Information

Before working with someone who will handle your investments or advise you what to buy, it's essential to check their background and qualifications. There are clear steps you can take:

Credentials and Registrations

Always ask for proof that advisers are registered with the proper financial authorities. In many countries, advisers must be licensed. In the US, for example, registration with the Securities and Exchange Commission (SEC) or the Financial Industry Regulatory Authority (FINRA) is required for many professionals.

Background Checks

Many countries provide free tools to look up financial advisers. In the US, you can check the SEC's Investment Adviser Public Disclosure website or FINRA's BrokerCheck database. These sites reveal if a person or company has a clean disciplinary record.

Questions to Ask

- What are your credentials and licenses?
- How are you compensated?
- Are you required to put my interests ahead of your own (fiduciary duty)?
- Can you provide references?

Reliable Information Sources

Be wary of viral articles, aggressive salespeople, or self-proclaimed experts without proven backgrounds. Trusted financial news outlets, government resources, and large, reputable financial institutions are safer sources for investment information.

Real-World Scams in Action

A retiree receives a phone call about a "can't-miss" overseas real estate deal, with promises of double-digit annual returns. The salesperson insists she must wire funds within 24 hours. Eager for secure income, she sends money — then never hears from the "firm" again. Or, a social media group hypes a little-known stock. Dozens of individuals buy in, the price surges for days, then collapses. The group moderators, the true orchestrators, disappear after cashing out at the top.

Steps for Due Diligence

Before making any investment, take deliberate steps:

- Research the company or adviser fully.
- Use databases to verify their identity and registration.
- Never invest under pressure; give yourself time to review details.
- Make sure you understand how the investment works and what fees are involved.
- Talk to others who have invested or seek advice from a third, unrelated party.
- Trust your instincts — if anything feels off, seek more information.

Table: Scam Red Flags vs. Legitimate Investments

Aspect	Scam	Legitimate Investment
Guarantees	Promised high, risk-free returns	Never guarantees
Pressure	Urgent, pushy to "act now"	Allows time for decisions
Registration	Unlicensed, can't provide credentials	Fully registered professionals
Clarity	Confusing, vague, or secretive	Explains details openly
Exclusivity	"Only for you," "once-in-a-lifetime"	Publicly available as an option

Trustworthy investments can always withstand your questions. Knowledge, skepticism, and careful research are your best shields against those hoping to trick you out of your hard-earned money.

Now that we understand the common emotional traps, hidden costs, and potential scams that can undermine our investing efforts, we are better equipped to make smart, confident decisions. By recognizing fear, FOMO, and panic before they take over, minimizing fees and unnecessary trades, and staying alert to red flags of fraud, we create a strong foundation for long-term success. With careful planning, patience, and a clear mind, anyone — whether just starting out or looking to grow wealth steadily — can navigate the investment world safely and build a brighter financial future.

NINETEEN
GROWING WEALTH OVER THE LONG TERM

Have you ever felt unsure about when to start investing or worried that putting money into the market at the wrong time could cost you dearly? Maybe you've wondered how some people manage to grow their savings steadily while others get stuck watching prices rise and fall, unsure what to do next. Building wealth over time can be confusing, especially if you're new to investing or balancing income from different jobs.

Many people face the challenge of learning how to make consistent, smart financial decisions without becoming overwhelmed by market ups and downs. Beyond simply choosing investments, there's also the question of how to plan for long-term goals like retirement, keep more of your earnings by managing taxes wisely, and track your progress without feeling lost or frustrated. This chapter focuses on practical ways to handle each of these areas, helping you build steady habits and strategies to grow your financial future with confidence.

EMPLOYING FOUNDATIONAL INVESTING STRATEGIES: DOLLAR-COST AVERAGING AND TAX-EFFICIENCY

Many people believe investing is risky because they worry about buying at the "wrong time." Dollar-cost averaging offers a simple solution. Instead of trying to predict when to invest, you decide to invest a fixed amount of money on a regular schedule, such as monthly or every paycheck. This method helps you buy more shares when prices are low and fewer when they are high. Over time, your average cost per share may be lower than if you tried to buy at specific times.

Imagine someone named Ana who decides to invest $100 at the start of each month in a global stock fund. In January, the fund price is $10 per share, so she buys 10 shares. In February, the price drops to $8, so her $100 buys 12.5 shares. In March, the price rises to $12, so she gets 8.33 shares. After three months, Ana has invested $300, and she owns 30.83 shares in total. Her average price per share is about $9.73, even though the share price fluctuated between $8 and $12. By spreading out her investments, Ana doesn't stress about timing the market perfectly.

Dollar-cost averaging works for investors at any income level. Whether you're investing $25 or $1,000 per month, the principle stays the same. This approach helps reduce the impact of sudden market swings and smooths out the ride, holding less risk than investing all your money at once.

Step-by-step Example of Dollar-Cost Averaging

1. Choose an amount you can comfortably invest each month (for example, $100).
2. Select an investment, such as a diversified stock or bond fund.
3. Set up automatic transfers so your money is invested on the same date each month.
4. Over time, record how many shares you buy each month.
5. Add up your total number of shares and the total amount invested. Divide your total investment by the number of shares to see your average cost per share.

By following these steps, you avoid buying everything at high prices and lessen the risk from short-term drops. This can be especially comforting during uncertain times.

Dollar-Cost Averaging: Up and Down Markets

Suppose prices fall for several months. With dollar-cost averaging, you'll end up buying more shares at lower prices. When the market eventually rebounds, the shares you have gathered at bargain prices can boost your returns. If prices rise steadily, dollar-cost averaging means your average purchase price climbs gradually as well, so you never spend all your money at the higher peak.

Mathematically, this method can be shown with a simple calculation. Let's say you invest $100 across four months, with share prices at $10, $8, $12, and $10. You buy 10, 12.5, 8.33, and 10 shares each month. Your total investment is $400, and you end up with about 40.83 shares. Your average price paid: $400 ÷ 40.83 ≈ $9.80. This average is lower than the highest price you would have paid if you invested all at once.

Why It's Ideal for New Investors

For newcomers, dollar-cost averaging lowers the stress of starting your investment journey. You don't need to be an expert or guess the best time to invest. Automatic investing also builds healthy financial habits, encouraging you to stick to your plan and grow your wealth over the long term.

Tax-Efficient Investing Strategies

Building wealth isn't just about investing but about keeping more of what you earn. Taxes can take a surprising bite out of investment gains. Tax-efficient investing helps you minimize that bite and allows your money to grow faster.

Every investor, regardless of country, can benefit from basic tax strategies. Start by using tax-advantaged accounts whenever possible. For example, many countries offer retirement accounts where your investments can grow tax-free or tax-deferred. In these accounts, you might not pay taxes on your investment returns every year; instead, you might pay tax only when you withdraw the money, hopefully in retirement when your tax rate may be lower.

Choosing tax-efficient investment vehicles is another important strategy. Index funds and exchange-traded funds (ETFs) tend to generate fewer taxable events because they buy and sell investments less frequently. Holding investments for the long term can also reduce your taxes, since many countries tax long-term investment gains at a lower rate.

How to Take Action

- Use retirement accounts and tax-free savings vehicles where available
- Favor lower-turnover funds, like ETFs or index funds.
- Hold investments longer to benefit from lower long-term tax rates
- Keep records of investments for easy tax reporting

Common Pitfalls

Many new investors forget about taxes until it's time to sell or withdraw funds. This can lead to unpleasant surprises. By considering taxes from the start, tracking contributions, and understanding your country's tax laws, you can avoid costly mistakes.

No matter your income or investment amount, dollar-cost averaging and tax-efficiency strategies help grow wealth steadily, setting the stage for future financial security and retirement peace of mind.

ALIGNING INVESTMENTS WITH RETIREMENT GOALS

Thinking about retirement might seem far off, but the choices made today have a real impact on life decades in the future. The key to financial safety in retirement is understanding the lifestyle you want and planning investments to make it possible. Start by asking simple but important questions: What age do you want to retire? Do you plan to travel? Will you downsize your home or move to a new location?

Will you have family or medical responsibilities to consider? Mapping out these details provides a clearer target for the amount of money needed.

Estimating living costs in retirement can be straightforward. List your expected monthly expenses, such as housing, food, healthcare, entertainment, transportation, and insurance. Add a buffer for unexpected costs — medical emergencies, home repairs, or changes in family circumstances. Use today's prices, but consider inflation. For example, if current expenses total $3,000 per month, plan for a 2–3% increase yearly to keep pace with rising costs. Multiply annual expenses by the number of years you expect to be retired; this gives a starting place for your savings goal.

After you've settled on a lifestyle estimate, figure out the investment return needed to reach this goal. Consider how much you can save each year and the number of years until you want to stop working. Online retirement calculators let you adjust for varying savings rates, inflation, and expected rates of return, showing how each factor affects your bottom line. For instance, saving $5,000 a year for 30 years with an average return of 6% will build nearly $400,000 before taxes. If cutting expenses or delaying retirement by five years increases your return or savings, it significantly boosts the final amount.

Choosing the right account for your retirement savings is just as important as the amount you save. Traditional individual retirement accounts (IRAs) and workplace 401(k) plans are popular. These accounts often allow pre-tax contributions, which lowers your taxable income now, although you'll pay taxes on withdrawals later. Roth IRAs and Roth 401(k)s let you contribute after-tax dollars, but withdrawals in retirement are tax-free. Freelancers and gig workers may use SEP IRAs or Solo 401(k)s, which offer higher contribution limits and flexibility.

Account Type	Contribution Type	Tax on Growth	Tax on Withdrawals	Who's Eligible
401(k)	Pre-tax/Roth	Tax-deferred	Taxed/Roth-free	Employees, some self-employed
Traditional IRA	Pre-tax	Tax-deferred	Taxed	Anyone with earned income
Roth IRA	After-tax	Grows tax-free	Tax-free	Those under income limits
SEP IRA	Pre-tax	Tax-deferred	Taxed	Self-employed, small business
Solo 401(k)	Pre-tax/Roth	Tax-deferred	Taxed/Roth-free	Self-employed

Choosing between these options depends on your tax situation, work status, and how much flexibility you need. A young professional might start with a Roth IRA for its tax-free growth and easier withdrawals in retirement, while a freelancer with variable income could benefit from a SEP IRA because of its higher contribution limits.

How you divide your investments among stocks, bonds, and cash — known as asset allocation — determines both your level of risk and potential returns. Younger investors can generally afford to invest more heavily in stocks, which carry higher risk but also higher long-term returns. As retirement nears, most people prefer to shift toward bonds and cash for more stability and predictable income. For example, someone in their twenties might use an 80% stock and 20% bond allocation, while a new retiree might hold 40% in stocks, 50% in bonds, and 10% in cash.

It's important to adjust this mix as you approach retirement, gradually reducing risk by shifting from stocks toward bonds and cash. Many investors choose target-date funds, which automatically adjust the allocation based on your expected retirement year.

Small mistakes can undermine years of careful planning. One common pitfall is ignoring inflation, which erodes the value of money over time.

Another is tapping into retirement savings too soon, resulting in penalties and lost growth. Underestimating healthcare costs is also risky. Avoid investing too conservatively early in your career, as this limits growth potential. Overestimating your ability to "catch up" later often leads to disappointment.

When you're finally ready to use your retirement savings, structure your withdrawals to last. Combining Social Security, investment income, and personal savings helps cover expenses. Many retirees use the "4% rule" — withdrawing 4% of their portfolio each year as income — to help make savings last roughly 25 years. Others opt for systematic withdrawals, annuities, or converting part of their investments to cash.

Consistent investment habits, smart account choices, the right mix of assets, and a willingness to adjust along the way put retirement goals within reach. Successful retirement planning means checking your portfolio and progress regularly and making necessary changes if your target or circumstances shift. This careful attention ties retirement security with ongoing performance tracking and ensures you'll stay on course as life changes.

TRACKING AND EVALUATING FINANCIAL PROGRESS

Watching your investments grow over time can be motivating, but successful long-term investors know progress requires more than checking account balances. An effective approach to measuring financial growth starts with selecting the right metrics, then setting up a system for tracking those metrics regularly — without letting emotions drive your decision-making. Productive tracking means monitoring your progress with clear, healthy routines, rather than reacting to every market bump or dip.

Key Performance Indicators for Long-Term Investors

Focusing on a few well-chosen indicators gives a clearer picture of progress. Net worth is a fundamental metric. This is the value of all your assets — like retirement accounts, investment portfolios, and real estate — minus debts. Tracking net worth over time shows whether you're moving closer to your retirement goal, even during periods of market volatility.

Annualized return is another essential indicator. It measures the average yearly gain or loss on your investments, smoothing out short-term ups and downs so you can see long-term trends. Portfolio growth relative to inflation is also important, since growth above inflation reflects real increases in purchasing power.

Asset allocation — the percentage of stocks, bonds, cash, and other asset types — is adjustable and should match your risk tolerance and time frame. Monitoring this balance helps ensure you stay invested in a way that reflects your goals.

Practical Tools and Tracking Methods

You don't need advanced software to monitor financial progress effectively. Many investors use spreadsheets to list accounts, assets, and debts, updating the sheet every quarter or twice yearly. Free online tools from brokerages and personal finance apps can link all accounts in one place and show net worth and performance at a glance.

Regular check-ins work best when you set planned intervals — monthly for checking overall account balances, quarterly for reviewing performance and asset allocation, and annually for a more profound review such as rebalancing. For example, you might review your portfolio performance and contributions on the first Saturday of every quarter and rebalance your investments every January.

A sample review schedule looks like this:

Interval	Actions	Why It Matters
Monthly	Check account balances	Stay aware, avoid surprises
Quarterly	Review returns, asset allocation	Keep on track with goals
Annually	Rebalance, set new goals	Adjust to life changes

Recognizing Warning Signs

Certain signs suggest it's time to review your plan outside of regular intervals. Large, unexpected changes in net worth that aren't tied to market swings, repeated failure to meet savings or contribution targets, or portfolio drift — where your actual investment mix is much different from your target — require a closer look.

In contrast, seeing your account balance drop during a market downturn isn't usually a cause for alarm as long as your investment approach matches your risk preference and time frame. Markets move up and down in the short term; what matters is the long-term trend.

Red Flags vs. Normal Behavior

Red Flags:

- Missing several planned contributions in a row
- Sudden, unexplained drops in net worth
- Asset allocation falling out of alignment significantly (e.g., stocks go from 60% to 80% of your portfolio)
- Strong urge to withdraw or radically change investments based on news headlines

Normal Market Changes:

- Seeing portfolio values fluctuate week-to-week
- Short-term underperformance compared to past years
- Several months of flat or negative growth during overall market corrections

Healthy Monitoring Habits and Avoiding Pitfalls

Healthy investors use scheduled reviews, not impulsive checks. Obsessively checking balances daily — or worse, multiple times daily — can lead to hasty, emotion-driven trades. A study habit is to check no more than once a month for balances and once a quarter for more profound reviews.

It's natural to feel uneasy during market drops, but anxiety can lead to selling at a loss or abandoning a well-planned strategy. Keeping a written investment policy helps; for example, note that your plan is long-term, with a set asset mix, and changes are only made during your scheduled annual review.

Setting Meaningful Benchmarks

Comparing your portfolio to a broad market index, like the S&P 500 for stocks or a balanced index for diversified investors, offers useful context. However, always relate benchmarks to your personal goals — like reaching a set nest egg by retirement age — rather than trying to outpace every market move.

The Role of Rebalancing and Handling Volatility

Rebalancing means adjusting investments to return to your target mix. If stocks rise sharply and become too large a portion of your portfolio, selling some and buying more of other asset classes keeps your risk level steady. Rebalancing once or twice a year is usually enough.

Finally, treat market volatility as normal. Remind yourself that short-term swings don't define long-term outcomes, and sticking to your routine is usually the best way to make progress toward your financial goals.

Now that you understand how proven investment strategies like dollar-cost averaging and tax-efficient planning work, you are better equipped to build steady, long-term wealth without the stress of market timing or unexpected tax surprises. By aligning your investments with clear retirement goals and consistently tracking your progress using simple tools, you can make informed decisions that keep you on course even when markets fluctuate. Remember, investing is a journey that rewards patience, regular habits, and smart adjustments as your life and goals evolve. With these methods in place, you can confidently take control of your financial future and watch your money grow over time.

TWENTY
YOUR INVESTOR MINDSET

Have you ever felt overwhelmed by the idea of investing, unsure where to begin or how to stay steady when markets swing wildly? Maybe you've wondered why some people seem to grow their wealth patiently over time, while others chase quick wins that come and go. It's easy to get caught up in daily price changes and headlines, losing sight of what truly matters for building lasting financial security.

The way you think about investing shapes not only your decisions but also your ability to stick with a plan through uncertain times. Developing the right mindset can transform investing from a stressful guessing game into a purposeful path toward your goals. This chapter invites you to explore how embracing long-term thinking, managing emotions, and connecting your investments to the life you want can set the foundation for success.

ADOPTING A LONG-TERM INVESTMENT PERSPECTIVE

Imagine you're choosing between planting a vegetable seed or buying salad from the store every day. Going with the seed takes patience — watering it, waiting, and watching it grow. Buying salad gives instant results but nothing for tomorrow. This is the difference between short-term and long-term investing. Day traders are like salad buyers, looking for quick gains by frequently buying and selling stocks. They focus on rapid swings, news headlines, and daily price changes, hoping to snatch small profits before moving on. Long-term investors, on the other hand, are gardeners. They buy shares in strong companies and hold those investments through sunny and stormy days, trusting that their value will rise over years, not minutes.

Long-term thinking isn't just about waiting; it's a mindset shift. Setting realistic timeframes is the foundation. If you're saving for a house in five years or building retirement wealth over decades, you tailor your investment plan to your unique timeline. It helps to write down specific goals: "I want to buy a home in 7 years," or "I'm building a retirement fund for age 65." These clear targets anchor you during volatile markets and help turn dreams into actionable plans.

One of the most powerful tools for long-term investors is compound interest. Think of it like rolling a snowball down a hill — it gets bigger faster the farther it travels. If you invest $5,000 at a 7% annual return and leave it alone, it grows not just from your original money, but from the earnings it makes each year. Over 20 years, that $5,000 can more than triple, all without you lifting a finger. The earlier you start, the bigger the snowball.

Price and value are often mistaken for the same thing, but there's an important difference. Price is what you pay for a share at any moment — like a sticker on a shirt at the mall. The shirt's value is its quality and longevity. Just because a stock's price drops or rises doesn't always mean its underlying value changed. Savvy investors look for quality companies that are underpriced relative to their potential, not just bargains on sale.

Emotions can sabotage even the best investment plans. When markets tumble, fear whispers, "Sell before it gets worse." When stocks surge, greed urges you to chase the hottest trend. Both can lead to costly decisions. Notice when your heartbeat rises as you check your investment app or when "doom-and-gloom" headlines get your attention. Taking a deep breath and remembering your long-term goals can serve as your initial defense.

Here are some actionable ways to build investment patience and discipline:

- Spend 15 minutes each week reviewing your goals instead of your portfolio's daily ups and downs.
- Create a simple habit: before making any investment move, wait 24 hours and write down your reasons for acting.
- Use automatic investing features to put away a fixed amount each month without thinking about market timing.

A helpful framework for decision-making is the checklist approach:

Simple Decision-Making Framework

Step	Action
1	Identify your goal and timeline
2	Research the investment's fundamentals (earnings, stability, history)
3	Ask if the price is attractive compared to its long-term value
4	Assess if the investment fits your broader portfolio
5	Pause, reflect, and then act rather than react

Consider these everyday scenarios:

A young professional opens a retirement account and consistently contributes a portion of every paycheck. Instead of jumping in and out of stocks based on market news, she trusts in the slow, steady climb of long-term growth. Years later, she finds her account much larger than friends who tried to time the market.

A freelancer enjoys irregular income. Instead of waiting for a big lump sum, he sets up an automatic transfer of whatever he can spare each month into a diversified fund. This keeps his investing habit alive, regardless of how busy or slow his business gets.

Someone with a side hustle decides that for every $100 earned, $20 goes into an index fund. Over five years, the discipline pays off, turning those small, regular investments into a solid nest egg.

Many worry that long-term investing means missing out on quicker money. However, research shows fewer trades often lead to lower taxes, decreased fees, and less emotional burnout. Market swings happen, but history demonstrates that patient investors who ride out volatility usually come out ahead.

Markets will always have ups and downs. Uncertainty is part of the journey, not a sign to panic. If you treat investing like planting a tree — nurturing it and waiting for its shade — rather than chasing every passing trend, you prepare yourself for healthier financial growth. wealthier future. Take small, thoughtful steps and trust in the process. The rewards build up, just like a seed becoming a tree.

NAVIGATING VOLATILITY & EMBRACING LIFELONG LEARNING

Markets move up and down for many reasons. Some days bring small, routine changes, while at other times larger swings can happen suddenly. This movement is called volatility. Volatility measures how much and how quickly prices change, and it comes in different forms. Normal volatility includes everyday ups and downs as investors react to news, company reports, or shifts in interest rates. Abnormal volatility, on the other hand, is less common and occurs during major events such as global crises or financial crashes, when prices move sharply in a short period.

Throughout history, the stock market has always moved in cycles. The financial crisis of 2008, the dot-com bubble burst in the early 2000s, and the COVID-19 market drop in 2020 all remind us that sharp declines can and do happen. Each time, investors who stayed patient eventually saw the markets recover. Successful long-term investors understand that downturns are part of the process. After most drops, markets have not only rebounded but often reached new highs, rewarding those who stayed invested. Recognizing the difference between short-term panic and lasting change is essential. A bad headline might send prices down briefly, but unless there's a deeper problem, it's usually just normal market movement.

When investments lose value, emotions can run high. Fear, anxiety, and frustration are common during market declines. These feelings can lead investors to sell at a loss or abandon their strategy altogether. Recognizing emotional triggers is the first step toward regaining control. Common triggers include seeing a negative account balance, hearing alarming news, or comparing losses with others. To manage emotions, pause and take a breath. Remind yourself why you invested and remember that downturns are temporary. Many investors use written plans to stay grounded, reviewing their long-term goals whenever fear starts to rise.

Several specific techniques can help maintain composure. Limiting how often you check your investment accounts helps avoid unnecessary stress. Setting up automatic contributions keeps your investment plan on track, even when headlines are dramatic. Another tool is "reframing": instead of seeing a drop as a loss, view it as a temporary dip and a possible buying opportunity. When in doubt, reach out to a mentor or a trusted advisor for perspective. Sticking to your plan, especially when it's tested by volatility, is one of the most powerful habits of successful investors. Research shows that most people who panic-sell regret it later, missing out on rebounds.

A simple framework for responding to volatility can make decisions easier during stressful times. Start with clear rules: decide in advance under what conditions you would make changes to your portfolio. For example, some changes are only warranted if your goals change, or if one part of your portfolio grows much larger than planned. Use checklists to avoid emotional decisions. Before acting, ask a few guiding questions: Did your financial needs change? Did something fundamental in the market or your investments shift for the long term?

Is this a rare, historic event or a normal part of the investment cycle? If the answer is no, holding steady is usually the smarter move.

Acting out of fear often leads to trouble, while disciplined investors benefit from patience. It's important to balance awareness with discipline. Occasionally, a major life change or a clear sign of trouble in a company or economy means you should adjust your plan. But most of the time, sticking with your original strategy works best. Reviewing your investments regularly — once or twice a year — is often enough. When in doubt, refer back to your personal investment goals, not the market's mood.

To make sense of what's happening without getting overwhelmed, rely on a few trusted information sources. Financial news from well-known sites, official market summaries, and reports from respected advisors can keep you informed. Ignore day-to-day noise from social media or opinion-based commentary that stirs fear or hype. Set time limits for reading market news and focus on data over drama. Write down important signals, such as changes to interest rates or official company updates. Limit checking portfolio values to a regular schedule — weekly or monthly instead of daily — to keep perspective.

Real-world examples offer proof that these strategies work. During the 2020 pandemic crash, investors who stayed invested through the drop saw their portfolios recover within months. Those who pulled out missed the upswing. Warren Buffett is known for his calm approach, famously saying to "be fearful when others are greedy and greedy when others are fearful." Many professionals avoid emotional pitfalls by sticking to decision-making frameworks.

Managing market volatility is a lifelong skill. Every cycle brings new lessons. Ongoing learning and reflection help you stay prepared, turning each market swing into a chance for growth and improvement as an investor.

USING INVESTMENT TO CREATE FREEDOM AND FULFILLMENT

Choosing to invest is about more than growing money. It's a way to build the kind of life you really want. When you step into investing, you adopt habits that reach far past your portfolio. Discipline, patience, and the drive to keep learning can shape your everyday choices, helping you become more intentional about life itself.

You may have already started asking yourself what truly matters to you. Begin simply. Set aside ten minutes with a notebook. List the moments in your life when you felt happiest, proudest, and most fulfilled. What do these memories have in common? Maybe you see adventure, family time, autonomy, or creativity popping up again and again. These patterns point directly to your core values.

Once you've prioritized your values, consider your most ambitious aspirations. Do you crave freedom to live anywhere? Time for creative projects? The security to weather unexpected changes? Turn these aspirations into clear statements. "I want to live in a new city every year." "I want to switch careers without worrying about my bills." "I want to retire while I still have energy to travel." When you can see the life you want in words, it becomes easier to map out the steps to getting there.

Translating values and aspirations into financial goals is next. If you desire location independence, you might set a goal of building a portfolio that generates steady passive income. Are you dreaming of an early retirement? Determine the amount you'll need to support your lifestyle, then break that number down into yearly savings and investment targets. An engineer who values flexibility could prioritize a sturdy emergency fund alongside investments in broad market index funds — tools that support smooth transitions if they want to take a career break or freelance.

Examples make the process real. Consider Maya, who loves travel and personal growth. She invests in dividend-paying stocks and real estate funds that provide regular income. She spends a few months each year living abroad, confident her investment income can support her adventures. Alex, seeking early retirement, follows a disciplined savings plan. He invests aggressively in tax-advantaged retirement accounts and automates regular contributions to keep on track. Instead of guessing, he calculates exactly how much he'll need each month and adjusts his portfolio every year based on his progress and changes in his goals.

Aligning your investments with your life vision isn't just for the wealthy or financial experts. Ordinary people constantly do this, in ways that fit their means and dreams. Parents who want to work less while their children are young might invest in rental properties. A freelance designer could build a small cash cushion before leaping into self-employment, investing the rest in low-cost funds to grow slowly over time. The goal is always the same: give your investments a job that serves your unique goals.

You can follow a clear process to keep your investing in sync with your life direction:

1. Identify your core values and aspirations.
2. Define specific lifestyle goals that reflect these values.
3. Calculate the financial requirements for each goal.
4. Choose investment strategies that best match your goals.
5. Set up automatic contributions or investment plans to stay consistent.
6. Review your progress and update your plan as needed.

Here's what this looks like in practice. Start with a worksheet or spreadsheet where you list each goal, the estimated cost, and the timeline. For example:

Goal	Estimated Cost	Timeline	Investment Strategy
Year-long world travel	$30,000	2 years	Short-term bond funds
Mini-retirement in 5 years	$120,000	5 years	Balanced mutual funds, CDs
Flexible remote work	$15,000	1 year	High-yield savings, ETFs

Every six to twelve months, revisit your sheet. Are your priorities changing? Did you reach one goal and now want to set your sights higher? Maybe your income increased, letting you invest more, or a new interest popped up that shifts your plans. Adjust your targets, rebalance your portfolio, and celebrate milestones along the way.

Building wealth is most rewarding when your money is doing more than multiplying on a statement. It's a tool for freedom, personal growth, and peace of mind. When you make investing a conscious part of your life design, you move closer to living each day on your own terms.

Start now. Reflect on what freedom and fulfillment truly mean to you. Make your list of core values and dreams, translate them into specific financial actions, and take that first step. Each dollar invested with a purpose is a step toward the life you envision.

Now that you understand the mindset needed for long-term investing, you can approach your financial journey with patience and confidence, knowing that staying focused on your goals will help you navigate market ups and downs without panic. By adopting habits like setting clear objectives, avoiding emotional reactions, and using automatic contributions, you create a steady path toward building wealth that supports the life you want. Remember, investing is more than just growing money — it's about creating freedom, resilience, and fulfillment in your everyday life. As you move forward, keep learning, stay disciplined, and trust in the process, knowing that every thoughtful step brings you closer to a secure and rewarding financial future.

YOUR FEEDBACK, THEIR FIRST STEP

Every time we share what we've learned, we light the path for someone else who may feel lost.

Have you ever wished you had clear guidance when you first started learning about money, investing, or building a financial future?

Imagine a young professional who wants to invest but feels overwhelmed by jargon, or a gig worker who wants to save for stability but isn't sure where to begin. For them, your perspective could be the spark of encouragement they need.

If *Investing 101* helped you feel more confident about investing — whether by simplifying the basics, showing you practical strategies, or helping you see that even small steps can lead to long-term growth — I'd be deeply grateful if you left an honest review.

Your feedback doesn't just help me improve; it helps future readers decide whether this book could give them the clarity and courage they need to begin their own journey toward financial independence.

Thank you so much for reading, reflecting, and — if you choose — sharing your thoughts. Your words have the power to guide others toward building the security and freedom they deserve.

CONCLUSION

You've reached the final page of this book, and it's a moment worth celebrating. Maybe you picked up these chapters feeling uncertain, maybe even intimidated — wondering if investing was only for wealthy experts or intimidating professionals in expensive suits. If you've ever thought that building wealth was something out of your reach, this journey should have painted a different picture: investing isn't about where you start — it's about moving forward, one step at a time, with confidence.

Over these pages, we've broken down the world of investing into its most essential pieces. You've learned that financial success isn't about luck, magical timing, or having a giant paycheck. It's built on consistency — showing up for your future self every day, even when it feels like your contributions are small. Simplicity is another foundational brick; you don't need to memorize complex stock charts or follow every twist and turn of the market. The best investors often focus on clear, simple decisions that work for them over time. And perhaps more important than anything else, you've discovered the value of trusting yourself. You can make good choices with your money, you can keep learning, and you can build a solid foundation — no matter where you're starting from today.

Think back to where you were at the beginning of this book. Maybe you saw investing as a winding, misty road filled with jargon and big risks. Now, you know that there's a path forward tailored to real, everyday people: students managing their first paychecks, gig workers collecting payments from multiple side hustles, young professionals balancing career steps with life goals, and anyone else who wants to put their money to work instead of watching it lose value in a checking account. If that sounds like you, know that you're exactly who this book was written for — and that you already have what it takes.

The tools and strategies you've picked up are designed to grow with you, no matter how complicated life becomes. Maybe you'll be working full-time, switching careers, freelancing, or juggling family obligations — all of these paths can support good investing habits. When you stay consistent, setting aside a small part of each paycheck, you send a powerful message to your future self: "I'm making my financial well-being a priority." This isn't about perfection — there will always be curveballs, months tighter than expected, markets that go up and down without warning — but every effort counts, and those little actions add up faster than you'd think.

If you remember just one thing from this book, let it be this: You do not need to have it all figured out before you start. In fact, no one does — not even the seasoned pros. What separates successful investors from everyone else isn't perfect timing or secret knowledge. It's a willingness to learn, to begin, and to course-correct along the way. Every investor, regardless of background or bank balance, has faced fears and doubts. But those feelings don't mean you shouldn't move forward. They're a sign that you care about your future, and that's a powerful motivator.

Don't wait for a perfect moment — because perfect moments rarely show up on schedule. Start with what you have, right now. Even small amounts, invested regularly, have the potential to grow impressively thanks to the power of compounding. Don't underestimate the impact of those first few dollars — or the momentum created by taking action. With every move you make, you gain new insight, confidence, and clarity. Over time, you'll see this process pay off, both financially and in your own sense of empowerment.

Investing isn't just about numbers on a screen or reaching some distant retirement goal. It's about freedom — the freedom to choose work because you want to, not because you have to; the opportunity to support causes you believe in; the ability to weather unexpected changes with stability and peace of mind. Each thoughtful decision you make today lays a stepping stone toward those possibilities.

Of course, your learning doesn't end here. If you're excited to keep going deeper, there are endless resources to help you sharpen your skills — books, podcasts, online courses, investment communities, and financial advisors who specialize in beginners. Seeking out trustworthy information is always a wise move, especially as the world of finance continues to evolve. Remember, staying curious and open-minded is what will keep you growing as an investor. Surround yourself with ideas and people who encourage your progress, not intimidate it.

One practical next step is to set a regular time in your calendar — once a month, or once a quarter — to review your investments and reflect on your progress. Track what's working for you, spot new opportunities, and celebrate your wins, no matter how small. If a certain strategy or tool isn't fitting your life anymore, give yourself permission to adjust. Investing should adapt to you — not the other way around.

For anyone still feeling nervous, trust that the hard part — getting started — is already behind you. You've chosen to educate yourself, to confront your fears, and to take responsibility for your financial destiny. That alone puts you ahead of the curve. While challenges may arise, the clarity and confidence you've gained will serve as steady companions on your journey.

Let's also acknowledge the courage it takes to challenge old ideas about money — perhaps ones you grew up with, or absorbed from pop culture and peers. Maybe you were led to believe that investing is risky, confusing, or only worthwhile if you already have plenty of cash lying around. By finishing this book, you've proven to yourself that you're ready to replace outdated beliefs with facts, strategies, and a genuine belief in your own abilities.

As you close these pages, hold tight to the main themes you've learned: the consistency of small, ongoing action; the beauty of simplicity — choosing investments and routines you understand and can stick with; and above all, self-trust. These qualities will carry you further than any trend or hot tip ever could. Your path will be unique, shaped by your values, responsibilities, and goals. There's no single formula, but there are timeless principles that work for everyone willing to apply them.

The best time to invest in your future is always now. Let this book be your launchpad, your primer, and your reminder that you are more than capable of turning your curiosity into concrete results. Whether you're a recent graduate, a freelancer, a side hustler, or someone simply looking for a better way, you have everything you need to get started — not someday, not after the next raise, but today.

Where you go from here is entirely up to you. Keep asking questions, keep seeking knowledge, and — most importantly — keep taking action. Let your first steps be bold, imperfect, and entirely your own. Investing is a lifelong journey, and you've taken the most important leap: you've begun.

Made in United States
Orlando, FL
04 November 2026

90202066R00125